FOOD TO GROW ON

FOOD TO GROW ON

GIVE YOUR KIDS A HEALTHY LIFESTYLE FOR KEEPS

SUSAN MENDELSON AND
RENA MENDELSON, M.S., D.Sc., R.D.

HarperCollins*PublishersLtd*

Food to Grow On
© 1994, 2005 by Rena Mendelson and
Susan Mendelson. All rights reserved.

Original paperback edition by HarperCollins
    Publishers Ltd: 1994
This revised and updated paperback edition: 2005

HarperCollins books may be purchased for educa-
tional, business, or sales promotional use through
our Special Markets Department.

HarperCollins Publishers Ltd
2 Bloor Street East, 20th Floor
Toronto, Ontario, Canada
M4W 1A8

www.harpercollins.ca

Library and Archives Canada Cataloguing in
Publication

Mendelson, Susan, 1952–
Food to grow on : give your kids a healthy
lifestyle for keeps / Susan Mendelson and
Rena Mendelson.

ISBN-13: 978-0-00-639508-9
ISBN-10: 0-00-639508-2

1. Children – Nutrition. 2. Cookery. I. Mendelson,
Rena II. Title.

RJ206.M45 2005   613.2'083   C2004-907071-1

KRO 9 8 7 6 5 4 3 2 1

Printed and bound in Canada
Set in Utopia and Formata

For our mother, Roz.
With love and admiration.

Table of Contents

PART ONE
BEFORE THE BEGINNING

PART TWO

INFANCY

PART THREE

CHILDHOOD

Foreword

On first glance, one might think that this is a cookbook with some nutritional rules for kids, or a nutritional rule book with some recipes. It is neither. It is a practical book, written by two people who have their own kids, have an excellent formal background in the principles of nutrition, and love to eat.

In my practise as a pediatric clinical nutritionist, I continue to be amazed that something as intuitive as feeding one's infant or child is so often seen by parents as mysterious and daunting. The result is parents who feel frustrated and guilty, and children who are over- or underweight and, as important, do not enjoy the process of eating. Susan and Rena Mendelson have recognized that the world of feeding one's offspring, literally from the moment of conception, is full of rules about what to eat, how to feed your child, how many helpings of this, and how many glasses of that. These rules, created by government officials and scientists, have taken the fun out of eating for many people, young and old. Susan and Rena's book not only takes the mystery out of meeting nutrient needs, but conveys the sense that eating can and should be fun. Their book clearly proclaims that getting kids to enjoy mealtimes involves much more than just the food that is presented to them.

The skills and experience of these two sisters is a wonderful combination. Rena has years of experience as a nutrition educator at Ryerson University and Susan as a cook and caterer. And, most important, these two women have intuitive smarts about food and behaviour. They recognize and address the complex relationship between the feeder and the individuals being fed. Food is much more than a combination of nutrients. It is often a reward and sometimes a punishment. It can be a source of pleasure and even a source of tension. This book recognizes the complexity of the behavioural components of eating and food, and incorporates this recognition both in the suggestions for getting kids and pregnant women to eat right, and in the recipes.

I cannot count the number of times I have told parents to feed kids only according to their appetite rather than insist that they clean their plates, only to be met with a blank stare of disbelief and disdain. Rena and Susan write, "Feed your child to meet her particular appetite; that is, do not force-feed her, but try to ensure that she gets enough calories to keep healthy. Of course this is easier said than done. I have encouraged each of my children to take just one more bite only to have them throw up on their plate after eating beyond their appetite. You really shouldn't mess with Mother Nature." By writing in a style that is personal (including anecdotes about their own kids and family) and extremely practical, they have managed to include the rules, but in a way that makes the reader forget they are rules.

Congratulations to Susan and Rena Mendelson, who have written a book that will be used by parents for years and years. This book truly is the children's version of Jane Brody's lifetime guide to good eating.

STANLEY ZLOTKIN, MD, PhD, FRCP(C)
DIVISION OF CLINICAL NUTRITION
THE HOSPITAL FOR SICK CHILDREN

Why We Wrote This Book

Ten years ago, we joined together our interests and expertise to create a resource for families. Susan brought her passion and flare for fabulous food. Rena brought her many years of research and experience teaching undergraduate university students about nutrition at critical stages of life. The end result was *Food to Grow On*, a single book with nutrition information from preconception to childhood and fantastic recipes for the whole family to enjoy. Since that time, nutrition and physical activity have dominated the headlines with growing concerns about childhood obesity and the health problems that children now face for the first time in history. These include adult-onset diabetes and elevated blood lipids, problems that were the domain of adults only ten years ago.

Our advice remains the same: set a good example through your own lifestyle choices, give children a variety of healthy foods, and do not use foods to punish or reward children. This revised *Food to Grow On* expands on that advice and adds information about the importance of physical activity from an early age. We have also included information about food safety and the updated nutrition recommendations.

We hope that you will find our advice and recipes a wonderful addition to your library and family dinner table.

SUSAN MENDELSON AND RENA MENDELSON

PART ONE

BEFORE THE BEGINNING

NUTRITION IS AN IMPORTANT PART OF HEALTH PROMO-
tion at every stage of the lifespan, but most
people would agree that it deserves special consideration
during the earliest stage of life. For this reason, no one
pays more attention to nutrition than expectant and new
parents. From this chapter you will learn about nutritional
needs and concerns not only during pregnancy, but also
during the time leading up to it. Because, believe it or
not, the impact of nutrition and health on pregnancy
begins before conception. Along with information about
the key nutrition issues, we have provided some exciting
and innovative recipes to help you put this information
to use.

Preconceptional Nutrition

If you're considering an addition to your family, you should be
concerned about nutrition and health before conception and during pregnancy. You'll have questions about both yourself and your
baby, from how much weight to gain to how much alcohol or coffee is safe to drink.

Some mothers tell themselves, "I will change my eating habits
when I know I am pregnant." This is usually applied to a whole set
of health behaviours such as smoking, alcohol consumption, exercise, and nutrition. For this reason, everyone in your family should

anticipate the pregnancy well ahead of conception and establish good eating and health practises. These positive lifestyle choices will help you provide a healthy environment for the protection and nourishment of your developing baby.

It is tough to make so many sudden changes to your lifestyle. Perhaps this is why some popular prenatal programs encourage women to apply even before they have conceived. These programs prepare parents for pregnancy both physically and emotionally. It makes sense to prepare ahead because most people never can tell when the critical moment of conception has taken place, marking the beginning of a new life. In fact, pregnancy may not be confirmed until some time after major development has already occurred.

Concerns about adequate growth before pregnancy used to be restricted to countries in which poverty is a major concern. However, North American dieting trends of the last two decades may have created a group of child-bearing women who have chosen to starve themselves for the sake of a fashionable look. The early dieting and food restrictions that young women endure through chronic dieting, anorexia nervosa, or bulimia may influence future generations by reducing the nutritional status of potentially healthy women to that of women who live in poverty. In fact, if early dieting experiences are prolonged, they can lead to fertility problems such as irregular menstrual cycles, cessation of menstruation (amenorrhea), or problems of conception. One survey of women attending a fertility clinic in Toronto revealed that more than half could be classified as having an eating disorder.

More and more attention is being paid to the health of

women who may become pregnant. This applies to warnings about workplace hazards, smoking, and drinking. Health Canada has advised all women who might become pregnant to increase their intake of the vitamin folic acid (also known as folate) in order to prevent neural tube defects. Since 1998, folic acid has been added to flour and cereals but this does not provide sufficient intake for all expectant mothers. Seek your doctor's advice about taking supplements.

The Effect of Birth Control Methods on Nutrition in Pregnancy

It comes as a surprise to many that during the first trimester of pregnancy (the first 12–14 weeks), the nourishment of the fetus will depend almost exclusively on the nutrients stored in the lining of the mother's uterus. Those nutrients were left there at least six months before conception. But it's never too late to change your diet, even after the pregnancy test comes back positive.

Various factors will have affected these nutritional stores. Obviously, diet is a major contributor. But body stores can also be influenced by the chronic use of drugs such as oral contraceptives or by birth control devices such as the IUD. Therefore, if you are planning a pregnancy, you should consider the effect of various types of birth control methods on your nutritional status. For example, if you have used an intrauterine device (IUD), you may have lost large amounts of blood during menstruation and may be slightly anemic. (In fact, most women are so low in iron stores that iron supplements are recommended as a routine for all pregnant women after the first trimester.) Or if you have been taking oral contraceptives for several years, you may have good iron stores but low stores of the B vitamins, such as folate, vitamin B_{12}, and vitamin B_6. (At one time, a clever vitamin manufacturer came up with the "pill pill," a vitamin supplement designed for women on the pill.)

The good news for women on the pill is that menstrual blood losses are lower with the pill and iron deficiency is less likely. In either case, it is probably a good idea to stop using IUDs or the pill at least six months before conceiving in order to increase your body's nutritional stores. Mechanical devices such as diaphragms or condoms and spermicidal jellies have no known effect on the nutritional stores for pregnancy.

Alcohol

Alcohol is the most widely used and abused drug in the world. If you tend to drink heavily, try to eliminate alcohol from your diet completely for a good six months before becoming pregnant.

In the early 1970s, a group of pediatricians in Seattle noticed that babies born to alcoholic women had similar facial features and similar medical problems. The facial features included narrow eye slits, which gave the appearance of a wide bridge across the nose. In addition, the babies did not grow at normal rates nor develop mentally beyond a certain level. The mental problems ranged from minor learning disabilities to profound mental disorders. Some of the children had heart problems and abnormal bone development. The pediatricians used the name fetal alcohol syndrome to describe the problem and began to look more closely at the causes. Before that time, there were no rigid alcohol restrictions imposed on pregnant women. Alcohol was actually prescribed to prevent premature labour.

The discovery of fetal alcohol syndrome caused a flurry of research activity to find out how widespread the problem might be, how much alcohol was safe to drink during pregnancy, and what could be done for children with the syndrome. Unfortunately, the damage is permanent. For this reason, some women have been charged with child abuse if they drank excessively during pregnancy. Some have even been denied access to their babies after birth. Although fetal alcohol syndrome appears to be more widespread than originally anticipated, it is unlikely to affect babies whose mothers have had only an occasional drink during pregnancy.

It is worth warning women to restrict their alcohol intake if they are considering pregnancy. For this reason, the federal government requires all manufacturers to place warning labels on alcoholic beverages. Moreover, women who consume one to two drinks of alcohol a day during the first and second trimesters have a higher rate of miscarriages. Research has also shown that alcoholic women who stop drinking immediately upon becoming pregnant are more likely to have underweight babies with medical problems, although these problems are greatly reduced compared to those who continue drinking. The best advice is to eliminate alcohol completely before pregnancy, although the occasional drink is unlikely to prove harmful.

Smoking

During recent years, smoking has been blamed for a number of early childhood problems. Mothers who smoke have babies who are significantly smaller than those of nonsmokers, and recent quitters have babies who are only slightly underweight. The reason that we worry about birth weight is that babies who are smaller than 5 lbs (3500 g) are at risk for a variety of health problems. One way of reducing these risks is to ensure healthy pregnancies and healthy birth weights. Smoking by mothers has been associated with sudden infant death syndrome (SIDS).

Women who return to smoking after the birth of the baby and fathers who smoke may also cause further problems through secondhand smoke. These include long-term respiratory problems as well as poor growth. Every member of the family should be aware of the need for lifestyle changes in anticipation of a new arrival. It's never too late to quit smoking. A smoke-free home will provide a healthier environment for your baby.

Weight Gain During Pregnancy

An overwhelming concern for those women who have struggled to keep their weights fashionably low is weight gain during pregnancy. How much is enough? How much is too much?

Weight gained during pregnancy is essential to meet the needs of the growing infant and the placenta, as well as to maintain the mother's nutritional stores in preparation for breast-feeding. Furthermore, we have come to realize the risks of low birth weight. We now know that it can be dangerous to produce a small baby.

Today's recommendations for weight gain suggest that women who enter pregnancy with a normal healthy weight should gain 25–35 lbs (11–15 kg) during pregnancy. A normal healthy weight is defined in a number of ways, one of which is through the body mass index (BMI). By marking your weight and height on the chart and drawing a line through the two points, you can get a reading for your own BMI. If the reading falls within the range of 20–27, you are considered a healthy prepregnant weight. Women who begin pregnancy with a low BMI (less than 20) are encouraged to gain 28–40 lbs (13–18 kg). On the other hand, women who enter pregnancy with a body mass index of greater than 27 are advised to gain 15–25 lbs (7–11 kg). Women who are expecting twins are advised to gain 35–45 lbs (16–20 kg).

The pattern of weight gain is just as important as the total amount gained. During the first trimester, weight gain should only be in the range of two to four pounds. From the second trimester until delivery, the expectant mother should gain weight according to her prepregnant BMI. If less than 20, she should gain 0.5 kg per week; if 20–27, 0.45 kg per week; if more than 27, 0.3 kg per week.

Body Mass Index

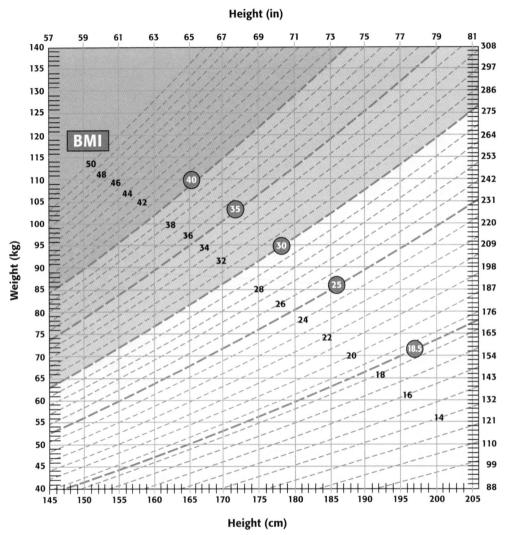

To estimate BMI, locate the point on the chart where height and weight intersect. Read the number on the dashed line closest to this point. For example, if you weigh 69 kg and are 173 cm tall, you have a BMI of approximately 23, which is in Normal Weight.

Source: Canadian Guidelines for Body Weight Classification in Adults. Health Canada. Ottawa, 2003. Reproduced with the permission of the Minister of Public Works and Government Services Canada, 2005.

These numbers should only be used as a guideline. In order to gain this amount of weight and to meet the high nutrient requirements, experts recommend that women rely on a variety of good-quality foods, eat to satisfy their appetites, and get regular amounts of moderate exercise.

Most women wonder how many calories it takes to gain this much weight. The total amount of energy required during pregnancy is estimated to use up an extra 300 calories per day or thereabouts. That's about one extra glass of 2 percent milk and one piece of buttered toast each day. Not much at all when you need to gain 30 pounds in nine months! The truth is that it is probably not quite so simple. The specific amount of energy required for women during pregnancy will depend on a whole set of factors including how much energy is spent on activities during this time.

It is important to think about weight before your pregnancy. For example, women who are obese or extremely overweight might be wise to watch their dietary intake to ensure that they are not eating excessive calories for several months before conception. Pregnancy is not the time for dieting or food restriction. (Following a low-carb, high-protein diet is not recommended.) Likewise, women who are significantly underweight should pay attention to their diets to ensure that they enter pregnancy at an optimally healthy weight.

Appetite

As we are too well aware, some women experience significant vomiting and nausea, which may lead to poor eating during the early stages of pregnancy. For most women, the discomfort lasts a few weeks only, but for others it can last much longer.

Once the early stages of pregnancy have passed, a new set of questions arise concerning appetite and weight gain. Now is the time to plan a "nutrient-dense" diet. This includes foods that have a high nutrient-calorie ratio. Remember, you are not really eating for two but rather for one and a bit. Some useful advice to keep you from overeating is to "eat to appetite." This means staying in touch with your body's true feelings of hunger and satiety. In other words, there is no reason to deny yourself food when you are truly hungry, but there is no need to overeat to gain the recommended weight. Besides, much of the weight gain is under the control of those hormones that take over during pregnancy. You may find that during the latter half of pregnancy your activities are reduced because you are uncomfortable and tire more easily. This will mean that you are using less energy and therefore need fewer calories for weight gain.

The weight gained during pregnancy will be lost some time after delivery. This generally holds true for women who have never had a so-called "weight problem." Unfortunately, the weight loss is not as rapid as most women would like and some patience is required. If you breast-feed, you will probably lose the weight gradually and without much effort as long as you are breast-feeding. This is because breast-feeding is an extremely energy-demanding activity and helps to burn off calories laid down during pregnancy. If you have a history of chronic dieting (the yo-yo syndrome), losing weight after pregnancy can be a continuation of your earlier battles. For some women, it becomes increasingly difficult with each pregnancy. The best advice is to prepare for the situation and come up with a specific plan to deal with it when the time comes.

Seek the help of a dietitian for this problem; don't take it on by yourself or with the advice of well-meaning friends.

Coping with Nausea and Vomiting

Women who experience extreme nausea and vomiting may be hospitalized to ensure they are getting adequate fluids and nutrients to keep them from becoming dehydrated. If you enter pregnancy with healthy nutritional stores in your body, you will be able to provide yourself and your baby with adequate nutrition even if you have a short period of poor eating or vomiting. But for most women who experience an average amount of discomfort, there are a few tips on coping with this unpleasantness. Some women find it helpful to eat a dry cracker before getting out of bed. Eating crackers between meals can also be helpful.

For many women the nausea and vomiting of pregnancy may pass within the first trimester. For others it may extend all the way through to the point of delivery. Small frequent meals may help to ensure comfort.

Another useful treatment is the use of Frozen Fruit Pops when nausea threatens. The cooling effect has its own merits and the fruit sugar helps to bring back blood sugar levels to a comfortable zone. Look for this recipe on page 266.

Nutrients of Special Concern During Pregnancy

Throughout pregnancy special attention needs to be paid to specific nutrients that play an important role in the development of the fetus and in the protection of the mother.

The tables in this section list examples of food and their nutritional value equivalents, providing the relative concentrations of certain vitamins or minerals for each group. While the amounts indicated may not reflect typical servings, the intended message is that all foods provide different concentrations of nutrients, so it is important to eat a variety every day to get the best possible nutrient value from your diet.

Calcium

Think of calcium as an expensive resource that can be deposited or withdrawn from your body's bank account. It is the most important mineral for the development of your baby's bones and teeth as well as the maintenance of your own bone mass. Pregnancy and breast-feeding both create very high demands for calcium because of the tremendous deposits required for a baby's development. These demands are made during pregnancy when the fetus is developing and growing; they are also made when the mother is manufacturing breast milk.

Although calcium is the most abundant mineral in the body, it is found in only a small number of foods. If your diet is too low in these foods, calcium is taken directly from your bones to supply it to the baby during pregnancy and to the milk during breast-feeding. Getting enough calcium from the diet becomes a double challenge for a woman who is less than 25 years old because her own bone mass is still increasing. Mothers who have several children in quick succession and provide them all with breast milk also run the risk of diminished bone mass if they do not sustain a very high calcium intake during this period of child-bearing. If they can't balance the calcium budget, women may be at high risk for calcium bankruptcy (in the form of osteoporosis) in later life.

Calcium is important not only for the development of bones and teeth, but also for muscles and their ability to contract. For example, the smooth muscle of the uterus and the lining of the arteries both rely on calcium for normal function. At one time women were instructed to take calcium to reduce leg cramps, but recent studies have shown that this is not necessary. Other studies have demonstrated that taking 1000–2000 mg of calcium per day may reduce blood pressure for pregnant women and lower the number of cases of high blood pressure brought on by pregnancy. Some (but not all) studies have suggested that there are great benefits from calcium supplements. In one experiment, the use of calcium supplements seemed to reduce the number of premature deliveries and the number of low-birth-weight babies. It is important to point out, however, that pregnancy-induced hypertension (high blood pressure), premature deliveries, and low-birth-weight babies are not caused by a deficiency of calcium alone.

Getting enough calcium during pregnancy by diet alone may seem challenging, but is as simple as getting at least four servings of dairy products a day. The recommended calcium intake during pregnancy is approximately 1000 mg per day. Each serving from the milk group contains 300 mg. Dairy products are ideal because they contain not only calcium, but vitamin D and lactose (or milk sugar), both of which help the body absorb calcium.

Mothers who do not consume dairy products because of lactose intolerance need to look at alternative ways of getting calcium into their diets and should discuss this with a dietitian for a strategic plan. Enzyme supplements may help digest lactose. You can also buy dairy products that have had the lactose removed. Several good products are available in supermarkets, including chocolate milk. In these products, the lactose sugar has been split into two by an enzyme during processing, which may make them taste sweeter than the regular products. Naturally processed yogurt and most ripened cheeses contain little or no lactose and provide a good amount of calcium for mothers-to-be. That is because the little microbes that ripen cheese and form yogurt use up lactose as they ferment these products. Ripened cheeses include Cheddar, Swiss, Edam, Gouda, Muenster, and brick. Cottage cheese and cream cheese are not ripened and might cause some discomfort to lactose-intolerant women. (In fact, cream cheese doesn't really belong in the same category with cheese at all. Since it is almost 50 percent fat, it should be considered in the same category as butter or margarine.) These two products are also rather low in calcium. In the case of cottage cheese, that is because the curds are separated from the whey, which contains calcium. Milk or cream added to the curds provides some additional calcium along with some lactose. However, dry cottage cheese has only a small amount of calcium to offer.

Some women may experience an improvement in their tolerance of lactose during pregnancy that allows them to consume more dairy foods without any discomfort.

Green vegetables such as bok choy and broccoli also provide

calcium. So do salmon, sardines, herring, and other canned fishes (with bones left in). Sesame seeds are another popular source.

Calcium supplements can also contribute to dietary calcium. Teenagers, mothers who are expecting twins or triplets, and previous dieters who may have a history of low-calcium diets may all be candidates for calcium supplements. Add to this list women with frequent pregnancies, as well as those with lactose intolerance. However, all would be wise to try to increase their intake of vitamin D as well as calcium. Be sure that the total amount of vitamin D in all of the supplements does not exceed 400 IU each day.

Women who are pregnant or lactating need four servings of high-calcium foods each day. Each serving should contain 300 mg of calcium. The recipes in this section give you a fun and delicious way to get it all. Calcium-rich recipes at the end of this section contain tofu, broccoli, cheeses, sesame seeds, and milk.

Good Sources of Calcium	Amount for 1/3 of Daily Need (300 mg)
Milk (any type)	1 cup (250 mL)
Cheddar cheese, shredded	1/3 cup (75 mL)
Parmesan cheese, grated	1 ounce (30 g)
Muenster cheese	1 1/2 ounces (45 g)
Bok choy, cooked	2 cups (500 mL)
Sardines, with bones	3 ounces (90 g)
Salmon, canned with bones	3 ounces (90 g)

Iron

Iron is extremely important for all of the changes taking place during pregnancy. It is an essential part of hemoglobin, which carries oxygen to each cell for energy metabolism. The increases in new tissue demand lots of iron. These include the developing infant, the increased blood supply to the placenta, and the increases in the mother's own body tissues.

Iron is perhaps the most common nutritional deficiency during pregnancy for North American women. Most women get barely enough iron before conception to sustain good body stores throughout their pregnancy. Many are on the verge of anemia. It's worth a routine blood test to find out if iron deficiency is causing problems of tiredness or fatigue. The need for iron during pregnancy is much higher than the usual requirement, so it's tough to get the necessary amounts without a supplement.

If you enter pregnancy with less than optimal iron stores in your body, you run the risk of developing anemia as soon as demands are made on those meagre stores. This is not just a problem that might occur during pregnancy. You can lose iron during surgery or other events that cause blood loss, such as accidents, extremely heavy menstrual flow, or bleeding ulcers. Therefore most women in North America can develop iron deficiency anemia at almost any time. All women should be evaluated for their iron status as a routine part of any regular medical exam, and especially during the early part of pregnancy.

The recommended intake for iron is hard to meet through a good diet alone. For this reason the United States National Academy of Sciences recommends that all pregnant women take 30–60 mg of iron a day in the form of a supplement from the twelfth week of pregnancy onwards. This supplement should ideally be consumed between meals to enhance its absorption. Iron supplements should not be consumed with milk, tea, or coffee, which are known to reduce the iron's absorption. In addition to the supplement it is a good idea for women to follow a diet that is high in iron. This includes meats and seafood such as clams and oysters, which not only provide their own source of iron but also enhance the absorption of iron from other sources. We have some great recipes for clams and mussels at the end of this section. One of the best-known foods for boosting iron intake is liver, but European health authorities advise pregnant women against the use of animal liver because sections of it may have toxic levels of vitamin A. Other iron-rich foods are peas, beans, nuts, dried fruits, and breakfast cereals.

You should be checked for anemia more than once during pregnancy to ensure that you are getting adequate amounts of iron from your diet and from supplements. If you test positive for anemia, you may have to increase your daily intake of iron to 50–120 mg. This could mean swallowing several pills every day. Taking one pill every few hours rather than all the pills at once will help you reduce the nausea, heartburn, diarrhea, and other discomforts associated with the use of an iron supplement. Because they may be better tolerated at bed time, take at least one of the supplements at that time.

Without iron supplements a woman may take up to two years to get her body stores back to normal. A good iron intake during pregnancy will also help to provide good iron stores for the baby. The baby's stores last for about four to six months after birth, when the infant begins to make his own supply of hemoglobin. Taking supplements will help to protect your baby as well as yourself from anemia.

Whenever we recommend a nutrient supplement, there is always room for some sort of caution. Just because "some is good" doesn't mean that "more is better." Never exceed the prescribed dosage. The use of a very high iron supplement as prescribed for women with anemia may also lead to a reduction in the absorption of zinc. If you take a supplement, eat the recommended levels of meat, poultry, and seafood to get an adequate level of zinc into your diet.

Good Sources of Iron	Amount for $1/3$ of Daily Need (6 mg)
Clams	2–3 clams
Beef steak, lean	6 ounces (175 g)
Prune juice	2 cups (500 mL)
Chickpeas	$1^1/4$ cup (300 mL)
Bagel (4 inch/10 cm diameter)	2
Breakfast cereals	1 cup (250 mL)
Shrimps	4 large
Lima beans	1 cup (250 mL)

Folate

Folate, also known as folic acid, is critical for the growth of all cells, especially the red blood cells, and for the development of new tissue. Some of the anemia that appears during pregnancy may be due to folate deficiency. However, folic acid supplements have been a concern in the past because their use may cover up a vitamin B_{12} deficiency known as pernicious anemia.

Low intakes of folic acid have been associated with neural tube defects (known as NTDs) in babies. The best known of these NTDs is spina bifida. Studies have shown that women who give birth to one child with an NTD have a better chance of giving birth to a child without one when they take folic acid supplements before and during pregnancy. As a result of these studies, Health Canada has recommended that all women at risk of pregnancy should take a supplement of 0.4 mg folic acid each day. Women with a history of NTDs may be advised to take ten times that amount (4 mg).

In 1998, Canada required that flours and flour-based products be fortified with folic acid. This adds 0.1 mg to our diet each day, which accounts for 25 percent of our daily needs. However, the recommendation for folate during pregnancy is twice the usual intake. Therefore it is worth knowing how to eat enough to ensure an adequate intake from foods. Good sources of folate include orange juice, vegetables such as dark green lettuce, asparagus, and broccoli, as well as peanuts and cereals. If you consume four of the following foods in the amounts listed, you can get the recommended folate intake from food each day.

The recipe section of this chapter has some excellent recipes for foods that are high in folate, including August Soup (page 59); Spinach, Romaine, and Strawberry Salad (page 63); Thai Spinach Salad (page 65); and Spinach and Tofu in Phyllo (page 105).

Good Sources of Folate	Amount for $1/4$ of Daily Need (100 mcg)
Spinach, fresh	$1^1/4$ cup (300 mL)
Romaine lettuce	$2^1/2$ cups (625 mL)
Broccoli	$1^1/3$ cups (325 mL)
Orange juice	$1^1/3$ cups (325 mL)
Chickpeas	$^1/3$ cup (75 mL)
Tomato juice	2 cups (500 mL)
Pineapple juice	2 cups (500 mL)
Wheat germ	$^1/4$ cup (50 mL)
Asparagus	5 spears

Vitamin B$_6$

Your need for vitamin B$_6$ increases during pregnancy because of hormonal changes. Nausea and depression have been associated with changes in vitamin B$_6$ metabolism brought on by PMS, pregnancy, or the use of oral contraceptives. Although B$_6$ deficiencies are rare, your doctor may prescribe a vitamin B$_6$ supplement to correct these symptoms. The prescription might be in the range of 5–10 mg a day, which far exceeds the normal requirement for vitamin B$_6$, but is well below the toxic dosage.

Some time ago patients taking their own prescriptions of one to two grams of B$_6$ (several hundred times the 5–10 mg prescription) were afflicted with permanent nerve and liver damage. Remember never to exceed the recommended dosage. In order to increase your intake of vitamin B$_6$, eat more vegetables, meats, and fruits.

Vitamin B$_{12}$

Vitamin B$_{12}$ is a special concern for women who have been strict vegetarians for more than a year. This vitamin is found mainly in foods of animal origin, such as milk, eggs, cheese, and meat. However, it may also be found in fermented vegetable-based foods such as miso, a fermented soy product. If you have not consumed these products for several years before pregnancy, you may require either a supplement or vitamin B$_{12}$ injections. Even if you have no symptoms of a deficiency of vitamin B$_{12}$ (anemia, weakness, or neurological problems), your baby may be born with inadequate stores to thrive during the first few months of breast-feeding. In one case in Los Angeles, a young infant who developed nerve damage in the first five months of life turned out to be suffering from a B_{12} deficiency. The deficiency was related to the vegan diet of the mother during pregnancy and breast-feeding. If you are a strict vegetarian, consult your doctor about B_{12} supplements.

Protein

Most women don't need to be especially concerned about getting adequate protein in their diets. In fact, most of us regularly eat twice the amount of protein we need.

In the early 1980s, researchers in New York City discovered that women taking protein supplements, in an effort to improve their babies' birth weights, actually had babies with lower weights. The reasons are not entirely clear, although it is fair to say that protein supplements are not recommended during pregnancy. However, if you are a very strict vegetarian, you should pay special attention to your protein intake. This could include careful blending of protein sources such as rice and beans or legumes and cereals to ensure that vegetable and grain sources offer the highest-quality protein. Combining complementing proteins will help you extend the protein value from vegetables and grains. Try the Easy Vegetarian Chili on page 77 or the Vegetarian Nut Burgers on page 103.

Zinc

Zinc plays a very important role in fetal development. Studies in Scandinavia suggested that a low zinc intake may be associated with an increase in the number of birth defects. This makes zinc a nutrient worthy of attention. If you are pregnant, you should be consuming meat, fish, seafood, and dairy products in order to get the best available sources of zinc. Oysters are an especially good source of zinc, however, fruits, vegetables, and grains provide only limited amounts.

There is no evidence to support the use of zinc supplements. In fact, mineral supplements can create problems, since several minerals use a similar route for absorption into the body. When too much of one mineral is available, it prevents others from being absorbed. For example, iron supplements can reduce zinc absorption and high zinc intake can compete with copper and iron. This is why you should never prescribe your own nutrient supplements. What appears to be a good thing may turn out to be harmful when used in excess.

Iodine

Iodine is an essential mineral for brain development, fetal development, and fetal survival, and was one of the first nutrients to be recognized for its role in causing birth defects when deficient. Although this is not a problem in North America, areas in the world where iodine is naturally deficient in the diet have very high numbers of babies born with cretinism. This syndrome includes mental retardation, abnormal thyroid function, and facial deformities. Since iodine supplementation has been introduced into these areas the number of infants born with cretinism has dropped. In North America, however, our diet is well supplied with iodine because we use iodized salt and eat foods with iodine-based preservatives in them.

Supplements

You will need multivitamin supplements if you're experiencing nausea and vomiting that keeps you from choosing a variety of balanced nutritious meals; if you have a history of weight reduction; if you are under twenty; or if you are expecting twins (or more!).

Supplements and other drugs that are not specifically prescribed for pregnancy can bring with them a set of potential complications. For example, the derivative of vitamin A called isotretinoin, which is used to treat cystic acne, has caused serious birth defects or spontaneous abortions when taken by pregnant women. Very clear warnings are printed on the labels of these products of vitamin A–like compounds about the dangers to pregnant women. Other fat-soluble vitamins may cause damage to the developing fetus; however, there are no cases reported.

If you take large doses of water-soluble vitamins, the fetus may become conditioned to high doses of the vitamin before birth. For example, taking megadoses of vitamin C throughout pregnancy may mean that your baby will need higher than normal amounts of vitamin C. The higher level of vitamin C that the infant was used to in pregnancy cannot be provided through breast-feeding. As a result, your child might be at risk of scurvy, a deficiency of vitamin C. Only take a supplement if your doctor considers it necessary.

Other Concerns During Pregnancy

Salt

You don't need to restrict your salt consumption during pregnancy unless your doctor advises you to. Water retention is part of the normal prenatal experience and a minimum intake of sodium between one and two grams is advisable. Since most people consume up to 10–12 grams of sodium a day, you will probably get more than adequate amounts of sodium in your diet throughout pregnancy.

Caffeine

Animal studies show that extremely high levels of caffeine can cause problems with pregnancy. However, studies on humans have demonstrated that caffeine is not something for pregnant women to be especially concerned about. Still, many people wonder how much caffeine is too much. Experts say that an intake of 400 mg of caffeine, equivalent to two to four cups of coffee per day is reasonable. This includes all of the caffeine that would be found in coffee, colas, tea, and chocolate, or in medications such as cough medicines. Restricting caffeine during pregnancy may be a useful exercise in preparation for breast-feeding, since caffeine gets into breast milk and may keep your baby awake. Beware of herbal teas, especially those with medicinal properties, as they may cause harm to you or your baby.

Heartburn

Heartburn is a problem that can develop at any point in pregnancy, but it may become noticeable after the nausea and vomiting subside. Typically it appears at about six months when the fetus is pressing against the diaphragm causing pressure on the stomach. Certain things, such as chocolate, will worsen the heartburn. Chocolate is a natural laxative that relaxes the upper passage into the stomach and allows the acidic contents to rise up and irritate the lower end of the esophagus.

If you use antacids to control heartburn, choose carefully. Calcium-based antacids can add to the total calcium intake and help to reduce the impact of heartburn at the same time. Although aluminum-based products may be effective in treating the symptoms, they may reduce the absorption of other nutrients.

Constipation

Constipation is a common problem during pregnancy and is caused by the changing levels of hormones. These hormones slow down the work of the digestive tract. The best way to deal with this is to increase the intake of fibre by eating lots of fruits and vegetables, high-fibre cereals, beans, and whole grains. Within each of these categories, there are certain foods that are particularly high in the type of fibre that will relieve constipation. Some examples are provided in the following table. Experts recommend 25–35 grams of fibre each day. Drink plenty of fluids and avoid laxatives if possible. They may create a problem of dependence, whereby the body loses its normal ability to pass waste. The most natural solutions are usually the best ones. We have included many delicious high-fibre recipes at the end of this chapter, such as White Bean Dip (page 48), Simple Lentil Vegetable Soup (page 56), and Rena's Berry Bran Muffins (page 209).

DIETARY FIBRE VALUES FOR FIBRE-CONTAINING FOODS

Food Group	Serving	Grams of Dietary Fibre
Breads and Cereals		
All Bran	⅓ cup (75 mL)	8.5
Oatmeal (cooked)	1 cup (250 mL)	2.2
Whole-wheat bread	1 slice	2.0
Vegetables, cooked		
Chickpeas	½ cup (125 mL)	6.0
Broccoli	½ cup (125 mL)	3.0
Carrots	½ cup (125 mL)	2.3
Green peas	½ cup (125 mL)	3.6
Parsnips	½ cup (125 mL)	2.7
Potato, with skin	1 medium	2.5
Lima beans	½ cup (125 mL)	5.0
Fruits		
Apple	1 medium	3.5
Banana	1 medium	3.0
Blueberries	1 cup (250 mL)	3.0
Orange	1 medium	3.0
Strawberries	1 cup (250 mL)	3.0
Raspberries	1 cup (250 mL)	8.0
Pear	1 medium	6.0

Cravings and Aversions

You may experience unusual cravings during different times of your pregnancy. There does not appear to be any nutritional explanation for these cravings. If you crave specific foods, indulge yourself, but try to eat other foods to balance your cravings. For example, if you crave meat and cheese sandwiches, be sure to get a salad, and fruit for dessert. If you crave sweets or salty chips, go ahead and have some, but eat them slowly and don't overdo it. A few women crave nonfoods like laundry starch or clay. These are potentially harmful for the digestion of other nutrients and should be avoided.

Food aversions may also create some concern. The odour or sight of foods such as raw meats may make you feel nauseated. If so, bring home prepared foods or opt for alternatives such as eggs, tuna, or cheese until the stage passes.

Food Safety

Two types of food safety practises are most important during pregnancy. The first is related to avoidance of environmentally contaminated foods and the second is related to food-borne illnesses.

Foods such as sport fish or game may have been contaminated by environmental exposure to heavy metals such as mercury or other industrial byproducts. For this reason, women are advised to avoid shark, swordfish, and king mackerel, and to limit their intake of fish caught by family or friends to six ounces per week. Fish oil supplements are not recommended because they may have similar contaminants and have not been tested for safety for pregnancy.

Food-borne illnesses are a common occurrence and may be misinterpreted as "stomach flu." They can create added distress during pregnancy and may even be dangerous to the developing fetus. To avoid them requires care related to food selection, storage, and preparation. Exposure to listeriosis can be especially dangerous during pregnancy. To avoid this, use only pasteurized dairy products, including cheeses; thoroughly cook all meat, seafood, poultry, and prepared meats (such as hot dogs, luncheon meats, and deli meats). Carefully wash all fruits and vegetables and avoid refrigerated pâté, smoked fish, soft cheeses, and meat spreads. During this time, it is best to avoid uncooked fish in sushi. Choose the

options that include cooked seafood such as shrimp or crab. Other forms of food contamination can be prevented by maintaining a clean food preparation area, including utensils, hands, and containers. In addition, it is important to store food at properly refrigerated temperatures and cook meats (especially ground meats), fish, and poultry thoroughly. Foods that are high in moisture and protein are especially vulnerable to microbial contamination and growth. If they remain at room temperature for two hours or more, the microbes will grow and multiply causing adverse reactions. The best rules of thumb are "keep hot foods hot and cold foods cold" and "when in doubt, throw it out."

Stress

The impact of stress on pregnancy has not been extensively examined. However, women under stress tend to have smaller babies and to deliver prematurely. Avoiding stress is easier to say than to do, but try to pace yourself, set reasonable goals, and learn to say "no" if your workload starts to get overwhelming. Try to maintain a healthy and normal routine and to present yourself in the most positive way. Some women really do blossom during pregnancy, others do not. Be fair to yourself and remember . . . this too shall pass.

Exercise

Many women are interested in continuing their exercise routines throughout pregnancy to enjoy the benefits of a healthy lifestyle. The effect of exercise on pregnancy has not been fully researched. However, there have been a number of elite athletes who continued training throughout most of pregnancy with good results. You need to know how your body is changing during pregnancy. For example, pregnancy will increase joint mobility and relaxation of the ligaments, which may increase your risk of sports injuries. You should also be aware of the risks of falls or other sports injuries when you are active.

Excessive exercise is a concern when it causes an increase in the core temperature of the body, since this could harm the developing fetus. For this reason, avoid saunas and steam baths, which increase your internal temperature. Even moderate exercise over a long period of time may decrease the amount of oxygen flowing through the uterus to the fetus. In general, use common sense in any fitness program and exercise within a level of comfort to ensure that you do no harm to yourself or to your baby.

Some good examples of exercises to carry on throughout pregnancy are swimming and walking. The key to maintaining a healthy level of activity is to feel comfortable throughout the exercise. Be sure to discuss any concerns you may have with your doctor.

BEFORE THE BEGINNING

RECIPES

THESE RECIPES WERE GATHERED FROM MANY CORNERS OF THE world and designed with the needs of the expectant mother in mind. The emphasis is on great-tasting food that is easy to prepare and is loaded with good nutrition. Each recipe is a practical and delicious application of the nutrition information we have presented. Nutrition highlights are provided for many of the recipes.

You might find yourself with an appetite for the most exotic or the most simple of foods. You may be more comfortable spreading your meals out to include midmorning and midafternoon snacks. You might find special comfort in the high-fibre foods designed with you in mind. The ideal foods to meet all of your special needs are in this section. But don't think of them in the same category as those maternity clothes you'll never wear again. These recipes are for now and always and will be a big hit with everyone in the family.

Using *Canada's Food Guide to Healthy Eating*, we recommend the following for pregnant or breast-feeding women:

Grain Products	9–12 servings a day
Vegetables and Fruits	8–10 servings a day
Milk Products	3–4 servings a day
Meat and Alternatives	2–3 servings a day

These amounts will add up to 1,735 calories for the lower number of servings or 2,300 calories for the higher number of servings. Adding oils or fats or sugars will add on calories without adding nutrients.

Grain Products

Canada's Food Guide to Healthy Eating recommends 5–12 servings of grain products each day. A serving is defined as one slice of bread, ⅔ cup (150 mL) cereal, or ½ cup (125 mL) pasta or rice. For pregnant or breast-feeding women, the upper end of this range is a reasonable goal, as long as you keep in touch with your appetite.

Ever since the recent popularity of Dr. Atkins's eating recommendations, the grain products acquired an unfounded reputation for being unhealthy and fattening. That was never true! Grain products are excellent sources of starch (important for energy) and fibre. Enriched and whole-grain products are especially good sources of iron and the B vitamins (niacin, thiamin, folic acid, and riboflavin).

Because grains are high in starch and generally low in fat, dietitians recommend eating more grains now than we have been eating. Eating more grains naturally causes us to eat less of the higher-fat foods. This should help us to change our meals to conform to the recommended shift to a lower-fat diet.

Plan meals around servings of breads, cereals, rice, pasta, or corn-based products. Add plenty of vegetables and fruits and a two to three ounces (50–75 g) serving from the meat and alternatives group. Planning meals to take on these proportions should help us to move creatively towards a healthier diet.

Look for other great grain recipes in Part 3.

Vegetables and Fruit

Canada's Food Guide to Healthy Eating recommends five to ten servings a day from the vegetables and fruit group. A serving is defined as one fruit or a ½ cup (125 mL) serving of vegetables. Like the grain products, these are good sources of carbohydrates, everyone's favourite source of energy. The guide also recommends that we eat dark green and orange vegetables as often as possible. This is because of their high content of folate, beta carotene, and minerals. Citrus fruits are also recommended because of the vitamin C content.

The benefits of fruits and vegetables cannot be overstated. New benefits are being discovered all the time. Foods of the onion family (garlic, onions, shallots) and the cabbage family (broccoli, cabbage, cauliflower, brussels sprouts) have received special attention. Lycopene from tomatoes and isoflavones from berries provide important health benefits. At this point, we are not recommending that you supplement your diet with the extracts of these foods, but that you make them an important part of your meal planning.

Vegetables and fruits can almost always be enjoyed in their raw form and should be eaten this way whenever possible. However juices and frozen and canned fruits and vegetables are also excellent sources of nutrients. The recipes in this section were designed to give you some exciting options to make vegetables and fruits a great part of your menu.

Milk Products

Milk products are the major source of calcium in the Canadian diet. In addition, they supply an important source of riboflavin, protein, and vitamin D. *Canada's Food Guide to Healthy Eating* recommends two to four servings a day and suggests that we choose lower-fat products more often. Pregnant and breast-feeding women need three to four servings a day. A serving size is defined as one cup (250 mL) milk, ¾ cup (175 mL) yogurt, or two slices of cheese.

Milk products include cheese, yogurt, and ice cream. Several of these foods have been combined in recipes with those of the other food groups. See the fruit soups with yogurt for additional examples. Many of the hot vegetable main courses include cheese and/or pasta or rice, giving you a two-in-one or three-in-one bonus.

If dairy fat is a concern, any of the recipes can be made with lower-fat cheeses, yogurt, or milk. There are more tasty varieties on the market every month.

Meats and Alternatives

The meat and alternatives group includes a wide variety of choices. Everything from meat, poultry, and fish to eggs and legumes belongs to this food group. Legumes are a group of high-protein, high-fibre seeds of plants. Some examples include peanuts, soybeans, lima beans, peas, and other beans. The products of these legumes, such as peanut butter and tofu, are also included. Tofu is derived from soybeans.

The recommended intake during pregnancy and breast-feeding is three servings a day. The serving size is defined as two to four ounces (50–100 g) of meat, fish, or poultry and one-half to one cup (125–250 mL) of beans. This is a portion about the size of a deck of cards. Consider the average restaurant serving size for some of these foods. The typical steak size of ten to sixteen ounces (250–400 g) may represent as many as four servings at one sitting!

This food group is a valuable source of many key nutrients. They include protein, fat, B vitamins (especially folate and B_{12}), and minerals (especially iron, zinc, and magnesium). The legumes also add an excellent source of lycopenes and fibre. We have provided recipes for a wide range of foods from the meats and alternatives that can be used as appetizers, soups, and salads, as well as main courses.

The following meal plan provides an example of a typical day using recipes from this book and the recommended number of servings found within each food group.

Breakfast

orange juice
⅔ cup (150 mL) Granola *(p. 45)*
Carrot and Banana Bread *(p. 43)* with peanut butter
1 cup (250 mL) milk

Snack

Apricot Bread *(p. 41)*
1 cup (250 mL) milk

Lunch

Carrot Ginger Soup *(p. 57)*
Easy Vegetarian Chili *(p. 77)*
Cornbread *(p. 216)* (2 slices)
peach slices with yogurt

Snack

Cheddar cheese on crackers

Dinner

New Wave Caesar Salad *(p. 64)*
Tomato Bruschetta with Roasted Garlic *(p. 46)*
Pasta with Sun-Dried Tomatoes and Vegetables *(p. 85)*
Red Snapper with Apricot Sauce *(p. 96)*
Triple Berry Crisp *(p. 110)*

Snack

fresh fruit salad

Apricot Bread

Fruit breads are a good source of starch and improve in flavour as they age . . . but don't be surprised if this one doesn't last very long.

½ lb (250 g) dried apricots	Chop by hand or in a food processor.
½ cup (125 mL) orange juice	Heat in large bowl in microwave, about 10 seconds on Medium.
¾ cup (175 mL) brown sugar	Add to orange juice. Add apricots and set aside.
2 eggs, beaten until frothy 3 tbsp (50 mL) oil ½ cup (125 mL) buttermilk	Combine.
2 cups (500 mL) all-purpose flour ¾ cup (175 mL) quick-cooking rolled oats, ground fine 2½ tsp (12 mL) baking powder ½ tsp (2 mL) baking soda ½ tsp (2 mL) salt	Mix together. Combine with egg mixture. Add egg mixture to apricot mixture.
½ cup (125 mL) chopped toasted almonds	Fold into batter.
	Pour into 9- x 5-inch (2 L) loaf pan and bake at 350°F (180°C) for 50–60 minutes, or until a toothpick inserted into the centre of the loaf comes out clean. MAKES ONE LARGE LOAF—10–12 SERVINGS.

Banana Pecan Bread

This is a great way to use up those overripe bananas and is a good source of starch and potassium.

¾ cup (175 mL) sugar 4 tbsp (60 mL) soft butter or margarine	Cream well.
3 medium bananas, mashed	Add to butter and sugar.
1 egg, beaten ⅓ cup (75 mL) buttermilk 2 cups (500 mL) all-purpose flour 1½ tsp (7 mL) baking powder ½ tsp (2 mL) baking soda ½ tsp (2 mL) salt	Mix together, then add to banana mixture.
1 cup (250 mL) chopped pecans	Fold into batter.
	Pour into 9- x 5-inch (2 L) loaf pan and bake at 350°F (180°C) for 1 hour, or until a toothpick inserted into the centre of the loaf comes out clean. MAKES ONE LARGE LOAF— 10–12 SERVINGS.

Carrot and Banana Bread

This recipe is a high-nutrition way to get rid of those overripe bananas. If you have several of them, make two loaves and freeze one.

³/₄ cup (175 mL) sugar 4 tbsp (60 mL) unsalted butter	Cream until fluffy.
2 large eggs	Add to creamed mixture, one at a time, and beat.
1 cup (250 mL) mashed bananas (about 2 medium)	Add to creamed mixture.
2 cups (500 mL) all-purpose flour 2 tsp (10 mL) baking powder ³/₄ tsp (4 mL) cinnamon ½ tsp (2 mL) salt ¼ tsp (1 mL) nutmeg Pinch ground cloves	Sift together and add to banana mixture.
³/₄ cup (175 mL) chopped walnuts ³/₄ cup (175 mL) grated carrots 1 tsp (5 mL) vanilla	Add to banana mixture and mix well.
	Pour into 9- x 5-inch (2 L) loaf pan and bake at 350°F (180°C) for 1 hour, or until a toothpick inserted into the centre of the loaf comes out clean. Let rest 15 minutes, then cool on rack before serving. MAKES ONE LARGE LOAF—10–12 SERVINGS.

Raspberry-Blueberry Cornmeal Muffins

Keep a muffin or two with you at work or when you are out and about. When you start to feel a little light-headed, nauseated, or hungry, this will help you make it to the next meal.

1 cup (250 mL) cornmeal 1 cup (250 mL) all-purpose flour ⅓ cup (75 mL) sugar 2 tsp (10 mL) baking powder ¼ tsp (1 mL) salt	Sift dry ingredients together in bowl.
1 cup (250 mL) buttermilk 6 tbsp (100 mL) melted butter 1 egg, lightly beaten	Form a well in dry ingredients and add combined liquids, stirring until just blended.
1 cup (250 mL) fresh or frozen blueberries ½ cup (125 mL) fresh or frozen raspberries	Fold in gently until just combined.
	Butter muffin tin, or use paper liners. Fill muffin tins ⅔ full. Bake 20–25 minutes at 400°F (200°C), or until tops of muffins spring back when lightly touched. MAKES 1 DOZEN LARGE MUFFINS.

Granola

Oats are a great source of soluble fibre. The nuts, seeds, and powdered milk make this a good source of protein. With a bowl of this for breakfast, you will feel sustained all morning long.

5 cups (1.25 L) quick-cooking rolled oats 1 cup (250 mL) chopped almonds 1 cup (250 mL) sunflower seeds 1 cup (250 mL) wheat germ 1 cup (250 mL) instant powdered milk	Mix together.
¾ cup (175 mL) liquid honey ½ cup (125 mL) vegetable oil	Heat together over medium heat until honey is runny, and add to oat mixture.
½ cup (125 mL) chopped dried apricots ½ cup (125 mL) raisins ½ cup (125 mL) chopped dates	Combine with honey-oat mixture.
	Spread onto 2–3 cookie sheets. Bake at 325°F (160°C) for 45 minutes, or until browned. MAKES 10 CUPS OR 20 ½-CUP SERVINGS.

Tomato Bruschetta with Roasted Garlic

A very flavourful hors d'oeuvre and also great for lunch with a green salad.

2 lbs (1 kg) tomatoes, peeled, seeded, and diced (about 6 medium)	Place in nonaluminum colander. Let drain 10 minutes. Put into large bowl.
¼ cup (50 mL) chopped basil 3 tbsp (50 mL) olive oil 1 tsp (5 mL) salt	Add to tomatoes and set aside.
6 cloves garlic, unpeeled 1 tbsp (15 mL) olive oil	Toss garlic and oil together, then place garlic on baking sheet. Roast at 375°F (190°C) for 10–12 minutes, or until soft. Cool slightly, then peel and chop coarsely. Toss tomatoes with roasted garlic.
1 baguette, diagonally sliced in 15 slices	Toast bread slices 30 seconds on each side under broiler. Remove from oven. Spoon 1–2 tbsp (15–25 mL) tomato mixture onto each slice.
⅓ cup (75 mL) grated Parmesan cheese (1 tsp per baguette slice)	Sprinkle 1 tsp (5 mL) Parmesan cheese on each slice. Return to oven for about 3 minutes, or until cheese begins to melt.
	MAKES 15 PIECES.

Imitation Liver

This is an unbelievably delicious hors d'oeuvre spread that has the taste and texture of Jewish chopped liver.

1 can (14 oz/398 mL) green beans	Strain beans and press out moisture.
1 large onion, chopped 1 tbsp (15 mL) olive oil	Sauté onion in oil.
3 hard-cooked eggs ½ cup (125 mL) walnuts 1–2 tbsp (15–25 mL) mayonnaise Salt and pepper to taste	Grind beans, onion, eggs, and walnuts in a blender or food processor with enough mayonnaise to make a firm mixture.
	Decorate with parsley and cherry tomatoes. SERVES 4–6.

White Bean Dip

White beans are high in fibre and protein, and low in fat. Serve with fresh carrot sticks, broccoli, green beans, celery, cauliflower, or tortilla chips.

1 can (15 oz/435 mL) white kidney beans, drained and rinsed 4 tsp (20 mL) lemon juice 3 cloves garlic, minced	Blend in food processor.
2 tbsp (25 mL) olive oil 1 tbsp chopped fresh parsley 1 tsp (5 mL) ground cumin ½ tsp (2 mL) chili powder Salt and pepper to taste	Add to bean mixture and process until blended.
1 tbsp (15 mL) minced cilantro	Sprinkle on top of dip. SERVES 4–6.

Mushroom Nut Pâté

The nuts and yogurt make this a high-protein, high-nutrient snack.

1 large onion, finely chopped 2 cloves garlic, minced 1 tbsp (15 mL) vegetable oil	Sauté onion and garlic in oil for 5 minutes.
1 lb (500 g) mushrooms, chopped 2 tbsp (25 mL) lemon juice 1 tsp (5 mL) dried basil ½ tsp (2 mL) dried thyme	Add to onions and garlic. Heat until liquid is completely reduced. Set aside to cool.
½ lb (250 g) walnuts ¼ lb (125 g) hazelnuts ½ lb (250 g) almonds	Toast nuts for 8 minutes at 350°F (180°C), then reduce to powder in a food processor. Set aside.
1 large bunch parsley, chopped 1 ½ cups (375 mL) yogurt 1 ½ tsp (7 mL) lemon juice ¼ tsp (1 mL) salt ¼ tsp (1 mL) pepper	Mix together in a large stainless steel bowl. Blend in food processor until smooth. Add onion and nut mixtures and process. Chill.
	Serve on whole wheat bread or crackers. SERVES 6–8.

Clams Steamed in Champagne

Clams are an excellent source of iron. One 3 oz (75 g) serving has 25 mg iron, which is almost as much as you'd get from an iron supplement. The iron in clams is also very easily absorbed. When champagne is heated, the alcohol disappears, leaving the flavour behind.

3 tbsp (50 mL) olive oil	Heat oil in heavy-bottomed pot.
½ lb (250 g) clams, well scrubbed 4 cloves garlic, minced	Add clams and garlic and cook for 2 minutes.
¾ cup (175 mL) champagne or sparkling white wine 2 green onions, finely chopped	Add wine and onions. Cover and steam for 5 minutes. Remove any unopened clams and discard. Remove remaining clams and set aside in a covered dish. Cook remaining liquid on medium-high heat for 5 minutes, or until reduced to ½ cup (125 mL).
2 tbsp (25 mL) butter	Whisk butter into liquid a little at a time.
2 tbsp (25 mL) chopped fresh parsley 1 tsp (5 mL) lemon juice	Add to champagne mixture. Pour mixture over clams and serve.
	SERVES 2.

Steamed Clams and Spicy Fennel

Chock full of iron and flavourful fennel, which has a subtle licorice flavour. Serve with crusty bread or on a bed of pasta.

2 tbsp (25 mL) olive oil	Heat in saucepan.
3 cloves garlic, minced ¾ tsp (4 mL) dried oregano ½ tsp (2 mL) dried basil ¼–½ tsp (1–2 mL) dried hot pepper flakes	Add to oil and cook over medium heat.
1 cup (250 mL) thinly sliced fennel bulbs ½ cup (125 mL) chopped onion	Add to garlic and herbs and sauté until fennel is softened (about 4–5 minutes).
1 can (14 oz/398 mL) plum tomatoes, chopped ¼ cup (50 mL) dry white wine	Add to fennel mixture and cook for 5 minutes.
30 clams, well scrubbed	Add to fennel and tomato mixture, cover, and continue cooking for 5–7 minutes, or until clams have opened. Discard any unopened clams.
	Serve on a platter and garnish with parsley. SERVES 2.

Saffron Mussels

Mussels are a good source of iron and zinc and an excellent source of folate and vitamin B$_{12}$.

½ cup (125 mL) chopped onion 2 cloves garlic, minced 1 tbsp (15 mL) olive oil	Sauté onions and garlic in oil until soft.
1 cup (250 mL) chopped tomatoes ½ cup (125 mL) white wine ½ cup (125 mL) water ½ tsp (2 mL) crumbled saffron	Add to onions and garlic and let simmer for 5 minutes.
2 lbs (1 kg) mussels, well scrubbed	Add to wine mixture and cover. Steam for 5–7 minutes, or until mussels open. Discard any unopened mussels.
	Serve with crusty bread. SERVES 2.

My Basic Vegetable Stock

Simmer soups gently on the lowest heat that will sustain a bubble. This will cut down on vitamin losses because a vigorous boil exposes them to more air bubbles, which cause destruction by oxidation. Feel free to throw in dried-up bits of carrots, celery, parsley stems, or onion.

3 qts (3 L) water 4 large carrots, peeled and cut in chunks 3 stalks celery, coarsely chopped 1 apple (unpeeled), cut in chunks 1 large onion, coarsely chopped 10 peppercorns 6 sprigs parsley 1 bay leaf	Wash all vegetables. Put vegetables and herbs in water and simmer for 45 minutes to 1 hour. Strain and use for making soup.
	MAKES 10 CUPS.

Pesto and Vegetable Soup

Carrots add beta carotene and fibre; chickpeas add protein and insoluble fibre; and broccoli adds calcium, beta carotene, folate, and vitamin C.

1 cup (250 mL) chopped onions 3 tbsp (50 mL) olive oil	Sauté onions in oil until soft.
2 carrots, chopped 1 small red pepper, seeded and chopped	Add to onions and sauté for 3–4 minutes.
5 cups (1.25 L) vegetable stock (see above) 1 ½ cups (375 mL) broccoli florets 1 cup (250 mL) chopped zucchini 1 cup (250 mL), cooked or canned chickpeas, drained and rinsed 1 cooking potato, peeled and diced	Add to onions, carrots, and pepper, and bring to a boil. Reduce heat and simmer for 15 minutes.
¼–⅓ cup (50–75 mL) pesto Salt and pepper to taste	Stir into vegetable mixture.
	SERVES 4–6.

Black Bean Soup

Black beans are a good source of starch, protein, and fibre. To balance the strong flavour of this soup, serve it with fresh rolls.

1 lb (500 g) dried black beans	Rinse beans 3 times and remove any stones. Put into a large saucepan.
5 qts (5 L) water ½ cup (125 mL) tomato purée 1½ tsp (7 mL) salt 1 tsp (5 mL) cumin 1 tsp (5 mL) dried oregano 1 tsp (5 mL) coriander seeds ½ tsp (2 mL) dried thyme 3 cloves garlic, minced	Add to beans and bring to a boil. Lower heat and simmer for 3 hours or until beans have softened.
	Take 2 cups (500 mL) of the bean mixture and purée in a blender. Return to pot. For a completely smooth soup, purée the entire contents of the pot. SERVES 6–8.

Minestrone Soup

A hearty soup. Feel free to throw in everything but the kitchen sink. This soup is a great opportunity to use up leftovers.

2 small onions, chopped 2 cloves garlic, minced 2 tbsp (25 mL) olive oil	In a large pot, sauté garlic and onions in oil for 3–4 minutes.
3 stalks celery, chopped 2 cups (500 mL) coarsely chopped zucchini 1 cup (250 mL) sliced mushrooms	Add to onions and garlic, and cook for 2–3 minutes.
10 cups (2.5 L) vegetable broth (page 53) 4 cups (1 L) peeled and chopped tomatoes 3 carrots, peeled and chopped 1 red pepper, seeded and chopped 1 tsp (5 mL) dried basil, or 1 tbsp fresh ½ tsp (2 mL) dried marjoram ½ tsp (2 mL) chili oil ¼ tsp (1 mL) dried thyme Bay leaf Salt and pepper to taste	Add to pot, bring mixture to a boil, then reduce heat and simmer for 25 minutes.
1½ cups (375 mL) cooked or canned chickpeas, drained and rinsed 1½ cups (375 mL) small pasta shells, cooked	Add to vegetables and herbs, and cook for another 5 minutes, or until chickpeas and pasta are hot. Ladle into bowls.
½ cup (125 mL) grated Parmesan cheese	Sprinkle 1 tbsp (15 mL) cheese on each bowl of soup.
	SERVES 8.

Simple Lentil Vegetable Soup

This soup makes a complete meal when you add bread, and fruit salad for dessert.

2–3 tbsp (25–50 mL) olive oil	Heat oil in large saucepan.
1 large onion, chopped 1 red pepper, seeded and chopped 3–4 cloves garlic, minced	Add to oil and sauté until tender.
8–10 cups (2–2.5 L) water 1½ cups (375 mL) lentils 1 cup (250 mL) brown rice, uncooked 1 cup (250 mL) dry white wine 2 cans (each 14 oz/398 mL) tomato sauce 3 large carrots, peeled and chopped 3 celery stalks, chopped 3 large red potatoes, peeled and diced 2 medium zucchinis, chopped 2 tsp (10 mL) dried basil 1 tsp (5 mL) dried thyme	Add to onion mixture. Cover saucepan and simmer about 1¼ hours, or until lentils and rice are tender.
	SERVES 8.

Carrot Ginger Soup

This soup is loaded with vitamins and minerals. We made this on The Journal *and got a great response. Eat the parsley too!*

6 cups (1.5 L) water 6 large carrots, whole 3 stalks celery, whole 1 onion, whole	Cook vegetables in 2-quart (2 L) saucepan for 15 minutes, or until carrots are tender. Remove carrots from liquid and place in blender with 2 cups (500 mL) of the cooking liquid. Blend until puréed. Set aside remaining water and vegetables for other uses.
1–2 cups (250–500 mL) buttermilk	Keep blender running and slowly add buttermilk.
1 tbsp (15 mL) grated gingerroot	Add ginger to blender. Return carrot-buttermilk mixture to saucepan and cook over medium heat until reheated.
	Serve with parsley sprigs. SERVES 4.

Broccoli Soup

This soup is an excellent source of calcium, beta carotene, and folate, and a good source of iron.

2½ lbs (1.25 kg) broccoli florets	Wash and cut broccoli into chunks. Microwave on high for 5 minutes. Set aside.
2 tbsp (25 mL) margarine	Melt in large saucepan over medium heat.
2 tbsp (25 mL) all-purpose flour	Add to margarine and stir for at least 1 minute.
3 cups (750 mL) 2% milk	Gradually add milk, stirring constantly until it reaches the boiling point.
¼ tsp (1 mL) grated nutmeg Salt and pepper to taste	Add to milk mixture. Pour all ingredients, including broccoli, into blender and blend until puréed. Return to saucepan.
1–2 cups (250–500 mL) vegetable stock	Add vegetable stock until desired consistency is reached and reheat.
	Serves 4–6.

August Soup

The cantaloupe and peaches are an excellent source of beta carotene, folate, and iron. Yogurt adds protein, calcium, vitamin B$_{12}$, and zinc. The alcohol content per serving is equal to the equivalent of one-sixth of an alcoholic beverage.

2 cups (500 mL) plain 2% yogurt

2 ripe peaches, peeled, pitted, and sliced

1 ripe cantaloupe, peeled and cut in chunks

2 tbsp (25 mL) amaretto liqueur (optional)

1 tbsp (15 mL) lemon juice

1 tsp (5 mL) almond extract

$\frac{1}{4}$ tsp (1 mL) cinnamon

Purée ingredients in a food processor or blender until smooth.

Chill 2–4 hours. Serve cold.

Serves 6.

Papaya Yogurt Soup

Papayas are a good source of iron and niacin, and an excellent source of vitamin C. Yogurt adds calcium, protein, and riboflavin.

1 lb (500 g) papaya, peeled, seeded, and cut in pieces

1–1$\frac{1}{2}$ cups (250–375 mL) 2% milk

1 cup (250 mL) plain 2% yogurt

3 tbsp (50 mL) sugar

Pinch cinnamon

Pinch grated nutmeg

Purée ingredients in a food processor or blender until smooth.

Chill 2–4 hours. Garnish with a slice of lime.

Serves 4.

Cold Beet Borscht

Beets are a good source of beta carotene and vitamin C and an excellent source of folate. The fat-free buttermilk adds calcium, protein, and riboflavin.

1 can (14 oz/398 mL) sliced beets 1 tsp (5 mL) sugar	Purée in blender or food processor.
2 cups (500 mL) buttermilk	Keep food processor or blender running and slowly add buttermilk.
Salt and pepper to taste Finely chopped cucumber 4 tbsp (50 mL) plain 2% yogurt	Add. Cover and refrigerate until cold (about 2 hours). Ladle soup into bowls and garnish with cucumber and a dollop of yogurt.
	SERVES 4.

Cantaloupe Peach Soup

Cantaloupe is a very good source of folate, beta carotene, and vitamin C.

1 ripe cantaloupe, peeled and cut in chunks	Purée in blender or food processor.
2 ripe peaches, peeled, pitted, and sliced ½ cup (125 mL) freshly squeezed orange juice 2 tbsp (25 mL) lime juice	Add to cantaloupe and purée.
4 tbsp (50 mL) plain 2% yogurt	Chill 1 hour. Garnish with a dollop of yogurt in centre of bowl.
	SERVES 4.

Gazpacho

The small amount of wine in this recipe should not pose any problems, but if you want the flavour and none of the alcohol, boil the wine for a few minutes, then cool it and add to the recipe. Alcohol evaporates when heated.

3 cups (750 mL) tomatoes, peeled and seeded

1 ½ cups (375 mL) chopped English cucumbers

1 cup (250 mL) tomato juice

½ cup (125 mL) chopped onion

2 stalks celery, chopped

1 red pepper, seeded and chopped

3 tbsp (50 mL) olive oil

3 tbsp (50 mL) red wine vinegar

¼ cup (50 mL) dry white wine

2 tbsp (25 mL) chopped fresh parsley

2 cloves garlic, minced

Juice of ½ lemon

Salt and pepper to taste

Purée in food processor or blender.

Refrigerate for 6–8 hours. Garnish with croutons and Parmesan cheese.

SERVES 8.

Bouillabaise

Serve with a spinach salad and multigrain bread.

1 cup (250 mL) leeks, chopped	Sauté leeks, onion, and garlic in olive oil.
1 cup (250 mL) onions, chopped	
3 cloves garlic, minced	
3 tbsp (50 mL) olive oil	
3 cups (750 mL) water or fish broth	Add to onions and garlic and simmer for 15 minutes.
2¹/₂ cups (625 mL) chopped fresh tomatoes	
1 cup (250 mL) dry white wine	
2 tsp (10 mL) crumbled saffron	
2 tsp (10 mL) dried parsley	
2 bay leaves	
¹/₄ tsp (1 mL) Tabasco sauce	
Salt and pepper to taste	
18 clams, well scrubbed	Add the seafood, bring to a boil, and simmer another 10 minutes. Discard any unopened clams or mussels.
12 mussels, well scrubbed	
¹/₂ lb (250 g) large shrimp, peeled and deveined	
¹/₂ lb (250 g) Alaska King Crab legs, chopped in pieces	
4 oz (120 g) scallops	
4 oz (120 g) fresh salmon, cut in chunks	
4 oz (120g) fresh halibut, cut in chunks	
2–3 tbsp (30–45 mL) Pernod or anisette	Before serving, add Pernod or anisette and stir.
	SERVES 4–6.

Spinach, Romaine, and Strawberry Salad with Poppyseed Dressing

This Winnipeg recipe is a popular salad in the winter when salads remind us of summer.

1 head romaine lettuce ½ bunch fresh spinach 1 cup (250 mL) sliced strawberries ¼ cup (50 mL) thinly sliced red onions	Wash, dry, and tear greens into bite-sized pieces. Toss together with strawberries and onions and set aside.
1 cup (250 mL) light mayonnaise ½ cup (125 mL) milk (2% or homogenized) ⅓ cup (75 mL) sugar ¼ cup (50 mL) raspberry vinegar 2 tbsp (25 mL) poppyseeds	Mix together to make dressing. Toss with salad.
	SERVES 6–8.

Corn and Bell Pepper Salad

Corn is a good source of starch and fibre, and is low in fat. Serve on curly red lettuce leaves.

10 oz (250 g) corn kernels, cooked and drained 1 red pepper, seeded and diced 1 green onion, chopped ½ green pepper, seeded and diced 2 tbsp (25 mL) chopped cilantro 2 tbsp (25 mL) olive oil 1 tbsp (15 mL) lime juice ¼ tsp (1 mL) cumin Salt and pepper to taste	Combine ingredients.
	SERVES 2–4.

New Wave Caesar Salad

We've combined spinach and romaine lettuce for more colour and texture than a traditional Caesar. The balsamic vinegar adds lots of flavour.

1 tbsp (15 mL) butter 2 tbsp (25 mL) olive oil 1 tbsp (15 mL) chopped fresh parsley 2 cloves garlic, minced	Melt butter in skillet, then add oil, parsley, and garlic and sauté.
8 slices French bread, cubed	Toss bread cubes in garlic mixture, coating thoroughly. Place on cookie sheet and bake at 350°F (180°C) for 10–15 minutes, or until crisp.
Dressing: ⅔ cup (150 mL) olive oil ¼ cup (50 mL) balsamic vinegar 1 egg, coddled in boiling water for 20 seconds 1–2 tsp (5–10 mL) anchovy paste 1 tsp (5 mL) Dijon mustard 1 clove garlic, minced ½ tsp (2 mL) salt ½ tsp (2 mL) pepper	Combine in blender and process well.
1 head romaine lettuce 1 bunch fresh spinach	Wash, dry, and tear greens into bite-sized pieces. Pour dressing over greens. Add croutons and toss.
½ cup (125 mL) grated Parmesan cheese	Sprinkle over salad.
	SERVES 8.

Thai Spinach Salad

Spinach is an excellent source of folate, calcium, and beta carotene. This is our favourite new salad. Try adding crunchy Chinese noodles for an even more exciting texture.

1 large bunch fresh spinach	Remove stems and wash well. Cut into ribbons.
1 cup (250 mL) fresh bean sprouts ½ cup (125 mL) slivered white mushrooms ½ cup (125 mL) slivered toasted almonds 1 red pepper, seeded and sliced	Toss with spinach.
Dressing: 3 tbsp (50 mL) lime juice ¼ cup (50 mL) peanut oil 2 tbsp (25 mL) brown sugar 1 tbsp (15 mL) minced fresh mint leaves, or 1 tbsp (15 mL) mint sauce 1 tbsp (15 mL) minced fresh basil 1½ tsp (7 mL) minced gingerroot ½ tsp (2 mL) Chinese chili garlic sauce Pinch grated nutmeg	Mix together. Pour over the spinach salad and toss.
	Serves 4–6.

Spinach Salad with Cashews, Apples, and Mango Chutney Dressing

This salad has all of my favourite ingredients. Feel free to experiment with different nuts. Toasted peanuts work beautifully and so do toasted almonds.

1 bunch baby spinach	Remove stems and wash well.
1 cup (250 mL) whole roasted cashews ¼ cup (50 mL) chopped green onion 1 tart green apple, coarsely chopped ½ mango, peeled and sliced	Toss with spinach.
Dressing: 2 tbsp (25 mL) lemon juice 2 tbsp (25 mL) mango chutney 1 tbsp (15 mL) red wine vinegar ½ tsp (2 mL) curry powder ¼ tsp (1 mL) sugar ¼ tsp (1 mL) salt Pinch cayenne pepper Pinch turmeric	Combine in blender and process for 2 minutes.
⅓ cup (75 mL) light vegetable oil	Keep blender going, and gradually add oil until mixture is smooth.
	Toss salad with dressing and serve immediately. Serves 4.

Vegetable and Wild Rice Salad

Perfect as a side dish for meat, poultry, and fish, or add a scrambled egg for a complete meal.

2 cups (500 mL) vegetable or chicken broth 1 cup (250 mL) wild rice	Bring broth to a boil. Stir in rice. Reduce to medium heat and simmer 1 hour, or until rice is tender.
2 cups (500 mL) broccoli florets ½ lb (250 g) asparagus, cut in small pieces diagonally ½ cup (125 mL) diagonally sliced green beans 2 medium carrots, peeled and sliced	Cook vegetables in a separate pot of boiling water until tender.
1 tomato, peeled, seeded, and chopped 4 oz (100 g) feta cheese, grated or crumbled	Combine with vegetables and rice and toss.
Dressing: 3 tbsp (50 mL) olive oil 2 tbsp (25 mL) lemon juice 1 tsp (5 mL) Dijon mustard Salt and pepper to taste	Mix together, and toss thoroughly with vegetables and rice.
	Serves 4.

Lazy Gourmet's Tofu Salad with Julienne Vegetables and Hoisin Sauce

Feel free to add any of your favourite vegetables to this salad. We've been making this at The Lazy Gourmet for years and customers have begged us for the recipe. Hope you enjoy it and that your kids do too!

Dressing: ½ cup (125 mL) black bean sauce ½ cup (125 mL) low-sodium soy sauce ½ cup (125 mL) hoisin sauce ½ cup (125 mL) balsamic vinegar ½ cup (125 mL) canola oil 2 tbsp (25 mL) sesame oil 2 tbsp (25 mL) sugar	Mix all ingredients together.
2 lb (1 kg) extra-firm tofu	Cut the tofu into 2- x 1-inch (5 x 2.5 cm) pieces.
2 tbsp (25 mL) canola oil	In skillet, fry tofu pieces in oil until golden on 2 sides.
2 cups (500 mL) julienned carrots 2 cups (500 mL) seeded and julienned red peppers 1 cup (250 mL) diagonally sliced green onions 1 cup (250 mL) diagonally sliced celery 1 cup (250 mL) diagonally sliced snow peas 1 cup (250 mL) shredded red cabbage	Mix the vegetables together and add dressing to taste.
	SERVES 6–8.

Couscous and Chickpea Salad

Easy to make! This dish has lots of fibre and protein, and is always a winner in our home.

1¾ cups (425 mL) water ½ tsp (2 mL) salt 6 oz (150 g) couscous	Bring salted water to boil. Add couscous. Cover. Remove from heat, and let sit for 5 minutes. Transfer to bowl and fluff with fork.
1 can (14 oz/398 mL) chickpeas, drained and rinsed 1 cup (250 mL) finely chopped carrots 1 large red pepper, seeded and chopped 4 green onions, chopped 4 tbsp (60 mL) chopped fresh parsley	Toss with couscous. Set aside.
Dressing: ½ cup (125 mL) mint leaves 3 tbsp (50 mL) lemon juice 1 tsp (5 mL) Dijon mustard ½ tsp (2 mL) sugar 1 clove garlic, minced	Blend in food processor or blender using on/off pulse.
½ cup (125 mL) olive oil	Gradually add oil to dressing while blending. Toss with couscous mixture. Serve on a bed of lettuce.
6 oz (150 g) feta cheese	Crumble on top of couscous.
	Serves 4.

Curried Chicken Salad

This is another often-requested recipe from The Lazy Gourmet. (The Lazy Gourmet is a takeout gourmet deli and catering company in Vancouver, B.C., owned by Susan Mendelson.)

2 cups (500 mL) diced cooked chicken

2 cups (500 mL) chopped celery

1 cup (250 mL) seeded and chopped red pepper

1 cup (250 mL) seeded and chopped green pepper

1 cup (250 mL) chopped mushrooms

½ cup (125 mL) coarsely chopped toasted almonds

½ cup (125 mL) red seedless grapes, halved

½ cup (125 mL) snow peas, lightly steamed

¼ cup (50 mL) chopped fresh parsley

¼ cup (50 mL) chopped red onion

Combine ingredients in a large bowl.

Dressing:

⅔ cup (150 mL) light mayonnaise

½ cup (125 mL) soft cream cheese

½ cup (125 mL) plain yogurt

2 tsp (10 mL) curry powder

1 tsp–1 tbsp (5–15 mL) liquid honey, to taste

2 dashes Tabasco sauce

Salt and pepper to taste

Whisk together in separate bowl until well blended. Toss dressing with salad.

Serve dressed salad in melon halves.

SERVES 8.

Yummy Cheese Enchiladas

We have a low-fat menu at The Lazy Gourmet called "café smart" and this is my favourite item from that menu. They're quick and easy to make.

16 6-inch (15 cm) corn tortillas	Wrap tortillas in foil and heat in 350°F (180°C) oven for 10 minutes, or until very pliable.
2 cups (500 mL) ricotta cheese 4 green onions, chopped 4 tsp (20 mL) lemon juice 1 tsp (5 mL) ground coriander ½ tsp (2 mL) cumin ½ tsp (2 mL) chili powder ¼ tsp (1 mL) cayenne pepper	Mix all ingredients together.
2 cups (500 mL) low-fat cheese	Assemble enchiladas with 2 tbsp (25 mL) cheese-and-onion mixture in centre of each tortilla. Fold in half. Place enchiladas in lightly oiled pan. Cover with foil and bake for 20 minutes at 350°F (180°C). Sprinkle with cheese (mozzarella, Swiss, or Monterey Jack). Bake an additional 4 minutes. Serve with Lazy Gourmet Salsa (see page 219) and plain yogurt.
	MAKES 16 ENCHILADAS.

Cauliflower, Broccoli, and Cheddar Kugel

Cauliflower and broccoli are excellent sources of folate. This dish makes a great main course. Start with Papaya Yogurt Soup (page 59) and fresh rolls, and finish with oatmeal cookies for dessert.

12 oz (300 g) egg noodles	Cook according to package instructions. Set aside.
3 tbsp (50 mL) vegetable oil 1 large onion, chopped 2 cloves garlic, minced	Sauté onion and garlic in oil until tender.
½ lb (250 g) mushrooms, sliced	Add to onions and garlic and sauté for 2 minutes, or until soft.
3 cups (750 mL) broccoli florets 3 cups (750 mL) coarsely chopped cauliflower	Microwave broccoli and cauliflower with ¼ cup water on High for 2 minutes, then add to mushroom mixture.
1 cup (250 mL) low-fat plain yogurt 1 cup (250 mL) low-fat cottage cheese 6 oz (150 g) Cheddar cheese, grated 3 eggs, beaten 2 tsp (10 mL) fresh basil, chopped, or 1 tsp (5 mL) dried basil 1 tsp (5 mL) dry mustard	Combine in separate bowl.
	Combine noodles, broccoli and cauliflower mixture, and yogurt mixture. Pour into 13- x 9-inch (3.5 L) or Bundt pan. Bake at 350°F (180°C), 35–40 minutes until golden on top. SERVES 6 AS A MAIN COURSE AND 8–10 AS A SIDE DISH.

Lynnie's Green Beans or Broccoli with Nami Sauce

This has a very rich flavour and makes you want to eat your greens! (Tahini will work if you can't find the Japanese product.)

2 lbs (1 kg) green beans or broccoli florets	Steam or boil or microwave until tender.
Nami Sauce: $^1/_3$ cup (75 mL) Japanese roasted sesame paste (or tahini) $^1/_4$ cup (50 mL) low-sodium soy sauce $^1/_4$ cup (50 mL) mirin (sweet rice wine) 2 tbsp (25 mL) roasted sesame seeds 2 tbsp (25 mL) rice vinegar 2 tsp (10 mL) sugar	Blend well with whisk. Pour sauce over vegetables.
2 tbsp (25 mL) roasted sesame seeds (optional)	Sprinkle on top. Serve.
	SERVES 6–8.

Spinach Orzo

Even our mother Roz, who shudders at the thought of spinach, loves this recipe and has been known to ask for seconds!

2 qts (2 L) water 2 cups (500 mL) orzo	Boil orzo in water for about 8 minutes or until tender. Set aside.
1 onion, chopped 3 cloves garlic, minced 4 tsp (20 mL) olive oil	Sauté onion and garlic in oil in large saucepan.
1 bunch fresh spinach	Wash spinach and cook until it is completely wilted. (It will be a little watery from the steam.) Process in blender until smooth.
4–6 tbsp (60–100 mL) grated Parmesan cheese Salt and pepper to taste	Toss Parmesan with spinach and orzo. Season with salt and pepper.
	SERVES 6–8.

Broccoli Soufflé

You can never have too many broccoli recipes. Broccoli is probably the all-time winner in nutrients. It is high in calcium, beta carotene, folate, and fibre.

3 cups (750 mL) broccoli florets	Steam broccoli for 5 minutes. Place in greased 12- x 8-inch (3 L) casserole.
1 small onion, chopped 3 tbsp (50 mL) butter	Sauté onion in butter until soft.
2 tbsp (25 mL) all-purpose flour	Add to onion and stir for one minute.
½ cup (125 mL) water Salt and pepper to taste	Slowly add to onion mixture and cook until thickened, stirring constantly.
3 eggs, beaten 2 cups (500 mL) grated Cheddar cheese	Add to onion mixture.
	Pour onion mixture over broccoli in casserole and bake at 350°F (180°C) for 40 minutes, or until firm in centre. SERVES 6–8.

Easy Broccoli and Tofu Sauté

This recipe offers a good combination of textures and is easy to make, and extremely tasty.

1 tbsp (15 mL) vegetable oil	Heat in nonstick skillet.
2 cloves garlic, minced 1 tbsp (15 mL) grated gingerroot	Add to oil and sauté for 2 minutes, or until soft.
2 cups (500 mL) broccoli florets	Microwave for 2 minutes on High with ¼ cup water, and add to ginger and garlic.
2 cups (500 mL) bean sprouts 1 cup (250 mL) sliced carrots	Add to broccoli mixture and sauté 1 minute.
¾ cup (175 mL) vegetable broth 2 tbsp (25 mL) low-sodium soy sauce 2 tbsp (25 mL) rice vinegar 1 tsp (5 mL) cornstarch 1 tsp (5 mL) Japanese sesame oil	Combine and stir to dissolve cornstarch. Add to broccoli mixture and cook 1 minute, or until tender.
¾ lb (375 g) firm tofu, cubed ½ cup (125 mL) diagonally sliced celery ½ cup (125 mL) diagonally sliced green onions	Add to broccoli mixture, cover, and cook for 1 minute.
	Serve with rice or pasta. SERVES 4–6.

Easy Vegetarian Chili

A delicious way to pump up the fibre. Add Spinach, Romaine, and Strawberry Salad with Poppyseed Dressing (page 63) as well as Polenta (page 78) or Cornbread (page 216) for a complete meal.

1 cup (250 mL) chopped onions 3 cloves garlic, minced 2 tbsp (25 mL) vegetable oil	Sauté onion and garlic in oil until softened.
1 red pepper, seeded and chopped 1 yellow pepper, seeded and chopped 1 green pepper, seeded and chopped	Add to onion and sauté for 3 minutes.
1 lb (500 g) pressed tofu, chopped in pieces	Add to pepper mixture and cook until browned.
1 can (28 oz/796 mL) crushed tomatoes 1 can (5½ oz/156 mL) tomato paste 3 tbsp (50 mL) chili powder 1 tbsp (15 mL) dried oregano 1 tsp (5 mL) salt ¼ tsp (1 mL) cayenne pepper ¼ tsp (1 mL) freshly ground pepper	Add to tofu and pepper mixture. Bring to a boil. Reduce and simmer for 30 minutes.
1 can (19 oz/540 mL) kidney beans, drained and rinsed 1 can (19 oz/540 mL) pinto beans, drained and rinsed 2 cups (500 mL) frozen corn kernels	Add and simmer an additional 30 minutes.
	Serves 8–10.

Polenta

Polenta is quick and easy to make and chock full of fibre and starch. It's perfect for family meals or for entertaining.

4 cups (1 L) water	Bring water to a boil in 2 qt (2 L) saucepan.
4 oz (100 g) yellow cornmeal	Stir in cornmeal and cook 5–6 minutes, stirring constantly. Remove from heat.
4 oz (100 g) Cheddar cheese, grated 1 tbsp (15 mL) margarine	Add cheese and margarine to cornmeal. Spray 15- x 10-inch (40 x 25 cm) jelly roll pan with nonstick spray. Pour in cornmeal mixture. Let stand 15–20 minutes.
2 tsp (10 mL) olive oil	Baste cornmeal with oil and bake at 450°F (230°C) for about 15 minutes, or until golden. Let cool slightly and cut into squares.
	MAKES ABOUT 20 SQUARES.

Spinach-Mushroom Gratin

I often vary the cheese and the toppings. I like to serve this with fish but it works well with everything, especially lamb and beef.

2 lbs (1 kg) fresh spinach leaves	Rinse spinach and steam or microwave until wilted. Drain well and squeeze out excess liquid. Set aside.
2 tbsp (25 mL) butter 2 leeks, thinly sliced (white and light green parts only) 2 cloves garlic, crushed 6 oz (180 gr) mushrooms, sliced	In saucepan, melt butter. Sauté leeks until soft. Add garlic and cook 1 minute. Add mushrooms and cook until just softened. Put the mixture into casserole dish
1 cup (250 mL) grated Parmesan cheese	Sprinkle over mixture.
2 egg whites 1 egg 1/2 cup (125 mL) milk Salt and pepper to taste	Put egg whites, egg, milk, and cooled spinach into food processor or blender. Add salt and pepper. Process well. Pour over mushroom mixture and use a fork to incorporate everything.
Topping: 1/3 cup (75 mL) crushed pecans 1/4 cup (50 mL) bread crumbs 1/4 cup (50 mL) grated Parmesan cheese	Mix together and sprinkle over spinach mixture. Bake at 350°F (180°C) for 25–30 minutes.
	SERVES 8.

Eggplant-Tomato Gratin

The key to this recipe is to bake the eggplant until it is soft. To me there's nothing worse than undercooked eggplant!

2 large eggplants 2–3 tbsp (25–50 mL) olive oil	Cut eggplants lengthwise, prick skin with fork. Place cut sides down on baking sheet. Baste with oil. Bake at 450°F (230°C) for 20 minutes or until tender. Let cool, then cut crosswise into ½-inch (1 cm) thick slices. Set aside.
1 can (28 oz/796 mL) plum tomatoes ¼ cup (50 mL) tomato paste 1 onion, finely chopped 2 cloves garlic, minced 1 tbsp (15 mL) dried basil 1 tsp (5 mL) dried oregano	Purée tomatoes, tomato paste, onion, garlic, and herbs in food processor. Pour into heavy pan.
1 large bay leaf	Add bay leaf to tomato mixture. Simmer uncovered for 20–30 minutes.
Freshly ground pepper	Season with pepper to taste. Remove bay leaf. Spread thin layer of tomato mixture in a 13- x 9-inch (3.5 L) baking dish. Cover with layer of eggplant. Continue to layer tomato mixture and eggplant until all slices have been used up.
1 cup (250 mL) shredded part-skim mozzarella cheese 2 tbsp (25 mL) grated Parmesan cheese	Top casserole with cheeses.
	Bake at 400°F (200°C) for 25–30 minutes or until bubbly. SERVES 6–8.

Laotian Rice
Baked in Banana Leaves

This is truly a sensational dish and very easy to make! Thanks to Lynnie again for another winner!

2 cups (500 mL) Thai fragrant rice	Cook as for Colourful Jasmine Rice (page 236) (without additional ingredients), and set aside.
5 lime leaves 2 green onions	Chop fine and set aside.
3 tbsp (50 mL) canola oil 1 tbsp (15 mL) crushed garlic	In large skillet, heat oil and garlic and cook until the garlic is brown and crispy but not burnt.
1/2 tsp (2 mL) Thai red curry paste 3 tbsp (50 mL) hot water	Add curry paste, turn down temperature and add hot water.
1/2 cup (125 mL) sliced mushrooms 1/2 cup (125 mL) seeded and finely chopped red peppers	Stir vegetables into sauce.
2 tbsp (25 mL) oyster sauce 1 tbsp (15 mL) low-sodium soy sauce 1 1/2 tsp (7 mL) freshly squeezed lime juice 1 tsp (5 mL) Thai curry powder 1/2 tsp (2 mL) sugar 1/2 tsp (2 mL) salt	Mix together, then add to skillet and stir until thickened. Stir in rice and lime leaf–onion mixture.
Banana leaves (one package, or about 3–4)	Line a 13- x 9-inch (3.5 L) casserole dish with the banana leaves and let the leaves extend 5–6 inches (12 cm) over the long edges and 4–5 inches (8 cm) over the ends. Place the rice mixture into the dish and wrap up with the banana leaves. Bake 350°F (118°C) for 35–40 minutes.
	SERVES 8–10.

Aida's Yams
with Marmelade Glaze

This is so simple and yet always gets great reviews. Any marmelade will do. We love lemon and pear!

4 large yams or sweet potatoes	Wash the yams and prick with fork. Wrap tightly with foil. Bake at 400°F (220°C) for 1 hour.
	Let cool. Remove foil. With paring knife, gently remove outer skin.
	Slice into $1^1/2$" (4 cm) thick slices and lay out in greased 13- x 9-inch (3.5 L) casserole dish.
$^1/_2$ cup (125 mL) marmelade—your choice $^1/_4$ cup (60 mL) orange juice	Mix together and brush or spoon gently over yams. Bake at 350°F (180°C) for 18–20 minutes until hot and marmelade sizzles.
	SERVES 8.

Roasted Potatoes with Rosemary

This is a garlic lover's dream come true. Feel free to experiment with different herbs. The garlic gets quite crispy, along with the potatoes. Make this recipe a day before you need it, since the flavours blend together wonderfully over 24 hours.

24 small nugget red potatoes, with skin	Cook potatoes in boiling water about 15 minutes, or until tender. Drain and cool. Cover and refrigerate at least 1 hour. Cut potatoes in quarters and put in large roasting pan.
⅓ cup (75 mL) olive oil 2 tbsp (25 mL) chopped fresh rosemary 12 cloves garlic, minced Salt and pepper to taste	Mix together and toss with potatoes.
	Bake at 375°F (190°C), tossing occasionally, for 45 minutes to 1 hour, or until golden and crisp. SERVES 6.

Linguine with Spicy Tomato and Clam Sauce

This recipe is packed with nutrients and is very satisfying. You can substitute mussels for the clams.

1 can (28 oz/796 mL) plum tomatoes	Drain in sieve. Chop into small pieces. Set aside.
2 tbsp (25 mL) olive oil	Heat oil in large skillet.
½ red onion, chopped	Sauté onion in oil until tender.
3 cloves garlic, minced 1 tsp (5 mL) chili garlic sauce or ¼ tsp (1 mL) crushed red pepper flakes (optional)	Add to onion and stir for 10 seconds. Add tomatoes to onion mixture.
2 tbsp (25 mL) chopped fresh parsley 1 tbsp (15 mL) fresh marjoram, chopped Salt and pepper to taste	Add seasonings to tomato mixture and simmer until thick (about 15 minutes).
1 lb (500 g) clams, well scrubbed	Add clams to tomato mixture and cover. Simmer 5 minutes, or until clams have opened. Discard any unopened clams.
½ lb (250 g) linguine	Cook pasta in boiling water until al dente. (Fresh pasta takes 7–8 minutes, dried pasta takes 10–12 minutes.) Toss sauce, clams, and linguine together, and divide into 2 bowls.
	SERVES 2.

Pasta with Sun-Dried Tomatoes and Vegetables

This is our favourite pasta dish.

4 cups (1L) cooked pasta	Set aside.
½ cup (125 mL) sun-dried tomatoes 2 cups (500 mL) boiling water	Soak tomatoes in water then cut into small pieces. Save water.
1 large onion 2 cloves garlic 1 tbsp (15 mL) oil	Chop onion and garlic and fry in small batches until dark brown. Add tomatoes and sauté.
1 chili pepper, cut in small pieces (optional)	Add to onion-garlic-tomato mixture, sauté 1 minute further, then toss with pasta.
4 cups (1L) total sliced snow peas, broccoli florets, sliced asparagus 4 tbsp (50 mL) Parmesan cheese	Steam and add to tomato water and toss with pasta. Add a little pepper. Sprinkle with Parmesan cheese.
	SERVES 2–4.

Linguine with Black Bean Sauce

This recipe was given to me by a chef specializing in fusion food or "East Meets West" cuisine. Everyone in my family loves it.

1½ tsp (7 mL) oil 1 small onion, diced fine	Sauté onion until soft in oil in large saucepan.
2 tbsp (25 mL) grated gingerroot 4–6 cloves garlic, minced 1½ tsp (7 mL) sesame oil	Add to saucepan and continue to sauté.
1 cup (250 mL) fermented black beans soaked in boiling water 5 minutes and rinsed twice	Process in food processor. Add to above and stir. Add a little water if you want it a bit smoother.
½ cup (125 mL) mushroom soy sauce ¼ cup (50 mL) oyster sauce ¼ cup (50 mL) water 1 tbsp (15 mL) sugar	Mix until smooth and add to bean mixture. Cook 3 minutes.
1½ lbs (750 g) linguine, cooked until al dente 2 cups (500 mL) broccoli florets, blanched ½ cup (125 mL) seeded, thinly sliced red pepper	Toss all ingredients together and serve hot.
	Add 1 tbsp (15 mL) finely chopped jalapeño peppers if a spicy flavour is preferred. Serves 6.

Carrot and Sweet Potato Tzimmes

This is a great accompaniment for a meat or chicken dish, full of beta carotene and fibre. I usually serve it for the Jewish New Year as it is sweet and everyone loves it.

2 lbs (1 kg) carrots, peeled and chopped 2 lbs (1 kg) sweet potatoes, peeled and cut in chunks	Cook carrots and potatoes in boiling water until tender. Set aside.
½ lb (250 g) dried prunes ½ lb (250 g) dried apricots	Place in a 13- x 9-inch (3.5 L) greased baking pan with the carrots and sweet potatoes.
1 can (14 oz/398 mL) crushed pineapple 3 tbsp (50 mL) liquid honey 3 tbsp (50 mL) melted butter Juice and rind from 2 oranges (optional)	Mix together pineapple, honey, butter, and orange juice and rind. Pour over vegetables and dried fruit. Bake at 350°F (180°C) for 30 minutes, stirring occasionally.
	SERVES 8–10.

Triple Bell Pepper and Onion Quesadillas

Quesadillas are fun to make and once you know how, you will have a great time experimenting with different fillings and cheeses. Serve with a salad for a terrific lunch, or serve alone with salsa for a great hors d'oeuvre. Corn tortillas are delicious and have more fibre than flour tortillas.

½ onion, chopped 1 tbsp (15 mL) vegetable oil	Sauté onion in oil until tender.
½ red pepper, seeded and finely chopped ½ green pepper, seeded and finely chopped ½ yellow pepper, seeded and finely chopped	Add and sauté until tender. Set aside.
4 oz (100 g) mozzarella cheese, grated 3 oz (75 g) goat cheese, crumbled	Mix together.
8 6-inch (15 cm) flour tortillas	Top four tortillas with ¼ of the onion-pepper filling and ¼ of the cheese mixture. Press a second tortilla gently on top of each one.
	Bake at 350°F (180°C) for 12–15 minutes, or until tortillas are crispy and the cheese has melted. Cut into triangles and serve with salsa. Serves 4.

Grandma Faye's Apricot Chicken

A Friday-night favourite of adults and kids in our house. It's an often-requested recipe at The Lazy Gourmet.

4 lb (2 kg) roasting chicken	Cut chicken into serving pieces. Remove skin. Set aside.
1 cup (250 mL) apricot jam ½ cup (125 mL) chili sauce ¼ cup (50 mL) dry white wine 2 tbsp (25 mL) low-sodium soy sauce 2 tbsp (25 mL) liquid honey 1 tbsp (15 mL) grated gingerroot ¼ tsp (1 mL) salt	Combine with a whisk in saucepan. Heat until well blended. Bring to low boil and remove from heat.
	Place chicken in large roasting pan. Baste thoroughly with sauce. Bake at 375°F (190°C) for 50–60 minutes, or until chicken is thoroughly cooked. If glaze is not sticky, pour it back into saucepan and cook until reduced and thick. Place chicken on plate and pour sauce on top to glaze. Serve with rice. SERVES 4–8.

Spicy Szechwan Chicken

This is great with Aida's Yams with Marmelade Glaze (page 82)
and Laotian Rice Baked in Banana Leaves (page 81).

Marinade:	Mix together.
3 tbsp (50 mL) dry sherry	
3 tbsp (50 mL) hoisin sauce	
3 tbsp (50 mL) low-sodium soy sauce	
2 tbsp (25 mL) oyster sauce	
2 tbsp (25 mL) balsamic or red wine vinegar	
1 tbsp (15 mL) sesame oil	
1 tbsp (15 mL) Asian chili sauce	
1 tbsp (15 mL) finely minced or grated gingerroot	
1 tbsp (15 mL) sugar	
4 cloves garlic, crushed	
2 green onions, minced	
2 frying chickens, cut in pieces	Rinse, pat dry, and place in bowl. Add marinade and coat evenly. Cover and refrigerate 3–4 hours.
	Roast chicken at 400°F (200°C) until juices run clear, about 30–40 minutes. Keep brushing with marinade during the roasting.
	If not brown when finished, put under broiler for 1 minute before serving.
	SERVES 6–8.

Soy Sesame Chicken with Oriental Vegetables

This chicken recipe can be eaten hot or cold.

Marinade: 6 tbsp (100 mL) low-sodium soy sauce ¼ cup (50 mL) chopped cilantro ¼ cup (50 mL) chopped green onion ¼ cup (50 mL) chicken or vegetable broth 2 tbsp (25 mL) grated gingerroot 2 tbsp (25 mL) rice vinegar 2 tsp (10 mL) hot chili paste with garlic 1 tsp (5 mL) sesame oil 4 cloves garlic, minced	Combine ingredients in bowl. Pour half of marinade into a separate bowl and set aside.
6 boneless, skinless chicken breasts, each about 4 oz (100 g)	Cover chicken with half of marinade. Refrigerate for 20 minutes.
1½ cups (375 mL) thinly sliced carrots 1½ cups (375 mL) snow peas, cut in threes 1 cup (250 mL) chopped broccoli florets	Cook vegetables with ½ cup (125 mL) water in microwave for 2 minutes on High.
1 tbsp (15 mL) peanut oil 1 tbsp (15 mL) sesame seeds	Heat oil in large skillet. Add chicken, smooth side down, and cook for 3–4 minutes. Turn and sprinkle with sesame seeds and heat for another 4–5 minutes, or until chicken is thoroughly cooked. Add the remainder of marinade and the vegetables, and stir until vegetables are done.
	Serves 6.

Halibut with Black Bean Sauce

I love to cook with fermented black beans. They can be found in Chinese food stores everywhere. Be sure to soak and rinse them well.

1 cup (250 mL) water 2–3 tbsp (25–50 mL) Chinese fermented black beans	Soak beans for 10 minutes in cold water, then drain and rinse. Place in small bowl.
2 tbsp (25 mL) low-sodium soy sauce 1 tbsp (15 mL) grated gingerroot 2 tsp (10 mL) sesame oil 2 tsp (10 mL) rice vinegar 3 cloves garlic, minced	Combine ingredients with beans and mash into paste or process in food mill.
1½ lbs (750 g) halibut or snapper fillets	Put rinsed fillets into lightly oiled 13- x 9-inch (3.5 L) baking dish. Spread bean paste over fillets. Cover dish with foil.
	Bake at 375°F (190°C) for 20–25 minutes, or until fish flakes. Serve with rice and green vegetables. MAKES 4 6-OZ SERVINGS, OR 6 4-OZ SERVINGS.

Halibut with Lemon Ginger Chili Marinade

Be careful not to overcook the halibut. I find that one minute too long can make a difference between a moist fish and a dry one. It's best to use fresh halibut for perfect results.

Marinade: ⅓ cup (75 mL) freshly squeezed lemon juice ½ cup (125 mL) dry white wine 2 tbsp (25 mL) canola oil 2 tbsp (25 mL) low-sodium soy sauce 1 tbsp (15 mL) finely minced lemon peel 1 tbsp (15 mL) finely minced or grated gingerroot 1 tbsp (15 mL) oyster sauce ½ tsp (2 mL) Asian chili sauce 2 cloves garlic, crushed	Mix together.
2 lbs (1 kg) halibut fillets, cut in 6 pieces	Marinate fish 15–20 minutes, turning to coat. Keep refrigerated until ready to cook. Broil 6" (14 cm) from element for approximately 10–12 minutes until fish flakes. Continue to coat with marinade as fish cooks.
	SERVES 6.

Sea Bass with Lime Ginger Sauce

Serve with mashed potatoes and steamed vegetables or Spinach-Mushroom Gratin (page 79).

Never tell anyone how easy this is. My family first had this in Mexico where our friend Michiko Sakata made it for us. It's another family favourite.

Because sea bass is fast becoming an endangered species, for the time being it is best to use halibut, sablefish, or snapper when making this recipe.

Sauce: 1 jar (8 oz/225 g) preserved whole ginger-root in syrup Juice of 2 limes	Process in food processor or blender.
8 pieces sea bass, each about 5 oz (150 g)	Place the fish on a broiler pan. Spoon the sauce on top (not too thick!). Broil 12 minutes until fish flakes and sauce caramelizes.
	SERVES 8.

Red Snapper with Tomato Basil and Garlic Sauce

Any white fish works with this recipe. The key is not to overcook!

2 cans (28 oz/750 mL) whole plum tomatoes	Process in blender or food processor. Place in a large saucepan and simmer uncovered until sauce is thickened.
Salt and pepper to taste	Add salt and pepper.
	Spray 13- x 9-inch (3.5L) Pyrex dish with cooking spray. Cut a piece of parchment the size of the dish and spray with more cooking spray. Set parchment and dish aside separately.
6 red snapper fillets, each about 5 oz (150 g) 2 tbsp (25 mL) dry white wine	Arrange the fillets in the dish. Sprinkle with wine.
½ cup (125 mL) vegetable or fish broth	Bring to a boil and pour over the fish. Put sprayed paper directly on the fish and bake at 425°F (220°C) 10–12 minutes. Remove the fish gently and pour the juices into the tomato sauce.
3 cloves garlic, minced Large bunch of basil, chopped fine	Add the garlic and basil to the tomato mixture. Boil until thickened again. Pour over the fish and serve immediately.
	Serves 6.

Red Snapper
with Apricot Sauce

I often serve this after I've rushed home from work and want an easy and special dinner. This sauce is also great as a last-minute sauce for chicken breasts. I just baste the chicken breasts and put them in a 375°F (190°C) oven for about 35 minutes. I also use this recipe for halibut.

1 ½ lbs (750 g) red snapper fillets Juice of ½ lemon	Rinse fillets and sprinkle with lemon juice.
½ cup (125 mL) apricot jam 3 tbsp (50 mL) low-sodium soy sauce 2 tbsp (25 mL) liquid honey	Mix together and brush onto snapper fillets.
	Place fish under broiler. Broil about 6 minutes on each side. Be careful not to overcook. MAKES 4 6-OZ SERVINGS OR 6 4-OZ SERVINGS.

Sablefish with Miso Glaze

Serve with Colourful Jasmine Rice (page 236) and steamed vegetables or Spinach-Mushroom Gratin (page 79).

This is our family's favourite fish. I serve it for fancy dinner parties and it always gets rave reviews. I never tell anyone how easy it is to make.

Marinade:	Combine in bowl. Mix well.
2/3 cup (150 mL) hoisin sauce	
1/3 cup (75 mL) white miso (shiro miso)	
2 tbsp (25 mL) sake	
2 tbsp (25 mL) fresh orange juice	
1 tbsp (15 mL) minced or grated gingerroot	
1 tbsp (15 mL) Asian chili paste with garlic	
4 tsp (20 mL) crushed garlic	
2 tsp (10 mL) brown sugar	
6 sablefish fillets, each 5 oz (150 g)	Add fish to marinade. Marinate 4 hours in refrigerator.
	Put the sablefish flesh-up on broiler pan, 6 inches (15 cm) below element.
	Spoon marinade on top. Broil 12 minutes until fish flakes and sauce caramelizes.
	SERVES 6.

Sole Rolled and Stuffed with Crab and Shrimp

This is a low-fat variation of a richer recipe that I make. I like it even better than the original.

1 ½ (20 mL) tbsp butter 1 onion, chopped 2 cups (500 mL) sliced mushrooms ½ cup (125 mL) chopped fresh parsley	Melt butter in frypan and sauté onion, mushrooms, and parsley.
3 oz (90 g) cooked crab 3 oz (90 g) cooked shrimp	Add to frypan and mix to combine.
6 sole fillets, each about 3 oz (90 g), skin removed 1 bunch fresh spinach lemon slices	With the sole fillets skinned side up, spoon mushroom-seafood mixture onto the fillets. Fold the fillets over the filling and arrange in a baking dish on a bed of partially steamed spinach with lemon slices on top.
	Bake at 350°F (180°C) for 15–20 minutes.
	SERVES 6.

Balsamic Soy Rack of Lamb

Great to serve with couscous or roasted potatoes and steamed vegetables.

2 racks of lamb (7–8 bones each)	Remove fat from top of racks. Using a paring knife, make a small cut between each bone to slightly pierce the meat.
Balsamic-Soy Marinade: ½ cup (125 mL) balsamic vinegar ½ cup (125 mL) dry red wine ⅓ cup (75 mL) reduced-sodium soy sauce 3 tbsp (50 mL) Dijon mustard 6 cloves of garlic, crushed	Combine and pour over lamb. Work the marinade into the slashes in the meat. Cover and refrigerate 4–6 hours.
4 tbsp (50 mL) honey mustard 2 tbsp (25 mL) mixed peppercorns—red, green, white, black—coarsely crushed	One hour before cooking mix and rub lamb racks with mustard and peppercorns. Roast at 450°F (230°C) until internal temperature is 140°F (60°C)—about 20 minutes. Let rest for 5 minutes, cut into chops and serve on heated platters.
	SERVES 4.

Beef Tenderloin with Black Bean Hoisin Sauce

We also cook this roast in the summer on the BBQ and it is fantastic! I recommend always using a meat thermometer to make sure that it is perfect (get one that reads Rare, Medium Rare, Medium, and Well Done). For vegetarians this is a terrific marinade for firm tofu that can be grilled or sautéed with assorted vegetables.

Marinade: 1 cup (250 mL) black bean sauce 1 cup (250 mL) reduced-sodium soy sauce 1 cup (250 mL) hoisin sauce 1/2 cup (125 mL) balsamic vinegar 1/4 cup (50 mL) sesame oil 2 tbsp (30 mL) sugar	Mix all ingredients together.
4 lb (2 kg) beef tenderloin roast	Marinate the roast in the sauce for 2–4 hours in roasting pan.
	Place in 500°F (260°C) oven for 5 minutes then reduce temperature to 425°F (220°C). Roast for 30–35 minutes until done to your liking. Let the roast sit for 5 minutes before slicing it. SERVES 10.

Vegetarian Loaf

I like to keep this around for a light lunch or sustenance to get me through an afternoon. I always feel healthy after I eat it and it's full of protein, fibre, vitamins, and minerals.

1 tbsp (15 mL) peanut oil	Heat in nonstick saucepan.
2 cups (500 mL) grated carrots 2 cups (500 mL) chopped mushrooms 1 cup (250 mL) chopped celery 1 cup (250 mL) seeded and chopped red pepper 1 cup (250 mL) chopped onion	Add vegetables and sauté about 5 minutes, or until softened.
2 cans (each 19 oz/540 mL) chickpeas, drained and rinsed 2 eggs	Combine eggs and chickpeas in food processor until coarsely chopped, and add to vegetables.
½ cup (125 mL) bread crumbs ½ tsp (2 mL) sea salt ¼ tsp (1 mL) pepper ¼ tsp (1 mL) cumin	Add to mixture and stir well.
	Press mixture into nonstick loaf pan sprayed with nonstick cooking spray. Bake at 375°F (190°C) for 30 minutes or until firm to touch. Serve hot or cold with Tzatziki (page 207). SERVES 6.

Falafel Burgers

These burgers are high in protein and fibre but low in fat. Deep frying is the traditional way of preparing falafel: these are baked.

¾ cup (175 mL) water	Bring to a boil.
2 oz (50 g) uncooked bulgur	Add bulgur to boiling water. Reduce heat to low and simmer for 10 minutes. Remove from heat and let stand 10 more minutes. Drain and transfer to large bowl. Set aside.
½ lb (250 g) cooked or canned chickpeas, drained and rinsed 2 tsp (10 mL) lemon juice ½ tsp (2 mL) cumin ¼ tsp (1 mL) sea salt ¼ tsp (1 mL) pepper 2 cloves garlic, minced	Process in food processor until smooth. Add to bulgur.
¼ cup (50 mL) bread crumbs	Add to bulgur mixture and mix well.
	Shape mixture into 12 large balls. Arrange on baking sheet sprayed with vegetable spray. Bake at 450°F (230 °C) for 15 minutes, or until lightly browned. Serve with Tahini Garlic Dip or Tzatziki (pages 205 and 207). MAKES 12 FALAFEL BALLS.

Vegetarian Nut Burgers

This is the hottest-selling burger at The Lazy Gourmet.

3 cups (750 mL) chopped walnuts

2½ cups (625 mL) bread crumbs

1 cup (125 mL) grated carrots

⅓ cup (75 mL) grated Monterey Jack cheese

⅓ cup (75 mL) sunflower seeds, hulled

½ cup (125 mL) vegetable oil

2 tbsp (25 mL) tamari or soy sauce

2 tsp (10 mL) crushed garlic

4 large eggs

Mix together thoroughly. (A food processor makes this easy.)

Form mixture into patties and grill, flipping to brown on both sides.

MAKES 8–12 PATTIES.

Lynnie's Couscous

Our sister Lynn often serves this to large crowds and always gets rave reviews.

¼ cup (50 mL) butter 2 medium onions, chopped	Sauté onions in butter until translucent.
1 cup (250 mL) chopped celery 2 tsp (10 mL) ground coriander 2 tsp (10 mL) cinnamon ¼ tsp (1 mL) cayenne pepper ¼ tsp (1 mL) crumbled saffron	Add to onion and cook additional 5 minutes.
2 lbs (1 kg) beef, cut in small cubes 2 cans (each 19 oz/540 mL) plum tomatoes 1 can (14 oz/398 mL) chickpeas, drained and rinsed 6 carrots, peeled and cut in chunks 4 turnips, peeled and cut in chunks 4 small zucchini, cut in chunks 2 acorn squashes, peeled and cut in small pieces 2 red peppers, seeded and cut in chunks 2 sticks cinnamon, cut in pieces 3 tbsp (50 mL) chopped fresh parsley	Add to onion and celery mixture and bring to a boil. Simmer for 30 minutes.
2 lbs (1 kg) couscous 8 cups (2 L) boiling salted water	Put couscous in water. Let sit for 5 minutes.
4 tbsp (60 mL) olive oil	Put oil in large skillet and toss with couscous for 5 minutes on medium heat.
	Serve vegetable and beef mixture over the couscous. SERVES 8.

Spinach and Tofu in Phyllo

This is a complete meal in an envelope.

1 large bunch fresh spinach	Wash spinach. Microwave 2 minutes on High. Squeeze out excess water and chop. Set aside.
2 tsp (10 mL) vegetable oil	Heat in large skillet.
1 cup (250 mL) chopped onion 2 cloves garlic, minced	Add to oil and cook until translucent.
1 cup (250 mL) seeded and chopped red peppers	Add to skillet and sauté 1 minute. Add spinach. Remove from heat.
2 eggs, beaten 3 tbsp (50 mL) grated Parmesan cheese	Mix eggs and cheese together and add to spinach.
½ lb (250 g) firm tofu, cubed 3 tbsp (50 mL) bread crumbs ½ tsp (2 mL) sea salt ¼ tsp (1 mL) nutmeg ¼ tsp (1 mL) pepper	Add to spinach and stir well.
6 sheets phyllo pastry	Spray each sheet phyllo with vegetable spray. Place ⅙ mixture on each sheet. Fold in sides and roll up into either log or envelope shape.
	Bake at 425°F (220°C) for 18 minutes, or until lightly browned. MAKES 6 ENVELOPES.

Tofu Burritos

This combination will provide all four food groups in one dish.

1½ lbs (750 g) medium-texture tofu (any tofu will work)	Cut tofu into 3 inch (7 cm) slices. Press excess water out of tofu by putting tofu on wire rack or cookie sheet and covering with flat casserole weighted with 3 or 4 cans. Let sit for 30 minutes. Drain and crumble tofu into bowl.
2 tbsp (25 mL) vegetable oil	Heat oil in large skillet.
2 cups (500 mL) chopped onion 3 cloves garlic, minced	Sauté in oil until tender.
1 or 2 jalapeño peppers, seeded and chopped fine 1 red pepper, seeded and chopped	Add to onion and garlic and sauté.
1 tsp (5 mL) dried oregano 1 tsp (5 mL) paprika 1 tsp (5 mL) ground coriander ¼ tsp (1 mL) chili powder	Add to peppers and cook for 2 more minutes.
1 cup (250 mL) frozen corn kernels, thawed 3 tbsp (50 mL) tomato paste 3 tbsp (50 mL) low-sodium soy sauce	Add to pepper mixture and stir. Add tofu.
6 10-inch (25 cm) flour tortillas	Spoon ¾ cup (175 mL) filling on centre of each tortilla. Roll up, enclosing filling. Spray 13- x 9-inch (3.5 L) baking dish with vegetable spray. Arrange tortillas in dish, seam side down. Spray with vegetable spray, and bake at 350°F (180°C) for 20 minutes, or until burritos are heated through. Serve with salsa and yogurt if desired. MAKES 6 BURRITOS.

Tofu with Red Peppers, Broccoli, and Snow Peas

This recipe takes minutes to prepare, and is very colourful, satisfying, and nutritious.

2 tbsp (25 mL) peanut oil	Pour into wok, heat, and swirl around.
2 cloves garlic, minced 1 tbsp (15 mL) minced gingerroot	Add to oil and cook 1 minute.
8 oz (250 g) tofu, cut in small squares 1 tbsp (15 mL) sake 1 tsp (5 mL) low-sodium soy sauce 1/4 tsp (1 mL) garlic powder	Toss tofu with sake, soy sauce, and garlic, and add to wok. Sauté until lightly browned. Remove to serving platter. Cover to keep warm.
1 cup (250 mL) broccoli florets 1 small onion, chopped 1/2 red pepper, seeded and chopped 1/2 cup (125 mL) snow peas	Put broccoli, onion, and pepper into wok and sauté until broccoli is bright green. Add snow peas at the last minute. Return tofu to wok.
2 tbsp (25 mL) low-sodium soy sauce 1 tbsp (15 mL) sake 2 tsp (10 mL) vegetable stock	Add to wok and simmer 1 more minute.
	Serve hot over steamed rice. SERVES 2–4.

Vegetable Fried Rice with Tofu

A meal in itself.

1 cup (250 mL) chopped onion 1 tbsp (15 mL) grated gingerroot 2 cloves garlic, minced 2 tbsp (25 mL) peanut oil	In wok or skillet, sauté onions, ginger, and garlic in oil.
1 cup (250 mL) chopped red cabbage 1 cup (250 mL) thinly sliced carrots 1 cup (250 mL) seeded and thinly sliced red peppers	Add and cook until cabbage softens.
3 cups (750 mL) cooked basmati rice	Add to cabbage mixture.
3 tbsp (50 mL) low-sodium soy sauce ¼ cup (50 mL) vegetable broth 1 tbsp (15 mL) sherry 1 tsp (5 mL) brown sugar ½ tsp (2 mL) chili paste ½ tsp (2 mL) sesame oil	Combine and add to cabbage-and-rice mixture.
¾ cup (175 mL) frozen peas	Heat peas for 1 minute in microwave on High. Then add to cabbage-and-rice mixture.
½ lb (250 g) tofu, cubed	Add to cabbage-and-rice mixture and heat until tofu is hot.
1–2 eggs (optional) 1 tsp (5 mL) vegetable oil (optional)	Quick fry eggs in oil in a skillet and add to tofu mixture.
	SERVES 4.

Apple Strudel

I make these in mini triangle versions for variety. The idea was stolen from a dessert served at a health spa in Arizona.

3 apples	Peel, core, and slice, and set aside.
5 tbsp (75 mL) brown sugar 1 tsp (5 mL) cinnamon	Mix well together and set aside.
6 sheets phyllo pastry Vegetable spray	Lay out one sheet of phyllo. Spray with vegetable spray for 1 second. Place ½ sliced apple along edge of phyllo. Sprinkle with ⅙ sugar mixture and fold over edges. Now roll up completely. Spray with vegetable spray. Place all 6 strudels in a 13- x 9-inch (3.5 L) baking pan and bake 400°F (200°C) for 12–15 minutes until golden.
	SERVES 6.

Blueberry Strudel Variation:

3 cups (750 mL) blueberries 6 tbsp (100 mL) sugar 1 tbsp (15 mL) cornstarch	Proceed according to above instructions with this blueberry filling.

Triple Berry Crisp

Take advantage of seasonal fruits to experiment with different variations on this recipe. This recipe started with raspberries, blueberries, and strawberries—but we thought the peaches added more flavour! We kept the original name. The topping is Rena's.

2 cups (500 mL) peeled, pitted, and sliced peaches 2 cups (500 mL) fresh or frozen raspberries 2 cups (500 mL) fresh or frozen blueberries ½ cup (125 mL) sugar 3 tbsp (50 mL) cornstarch ¼ tsp (1 mL) nutmeg	Mix together in large bowl and turn into 9-inch (23 cm) pie plate. Set aside.
¾ cup (175 mL) quick-cooking rolled oats ½ cup (125 mL) brown sugar ⅓ cup (75 mL) cold butter or margarine ¼ cup (50 mL) flax seed ¼ cup (50 mL) wheat germ ¼ cup (50 mL) bran	Rub together to form crumb topping. Spread over berries.
	Place pie pan on cookie sheet (to catch extra juice) and bake at 350°F (180°C) for 30–40 minutes. SERVES 6.

Honey Biscotti

This is a wonderful low-fat snack. The traditional biscotti are extremely crunchy, so be forewarned. I especially like them because each cookie takes about 10 minutes to eat! This is not a cookie for kids.

1 ¼ cup (300 mL) whole almonds	Toast almonds for 10 minutes in 375°F (190°C) oven and set aside.
3 large eggs, beaten ½ cup (125 mL) liquid honey 1 tsp (5 mL) vanilla ½ tsp (2 mL) licorice flavouring	Combine and mix well. Set aside.
3 cups (750 mL) all-purpose flour ½ cup (125 mL) granulated sugar 1 tsp (5 mL) baking powder ½ tsp (2 mL) white pepper ½ tsp (2 mL) ground ginger ¼ tsp (1 mL) salt	Sift dry ingredients together. Add egg mixture all at once. Beat with electric beater on low speed until dough holds together. Fold in almonds.
	Lightly flour a large work surface and turn dough out onto the floured area. Sift ¼ cup (50 mL) flour over top of dough. Shape into 3 logs. Bake 50 minutes at 300°F (150°C), then slice into diagonals. Place cookies cut side down on cookie sheet, reduce oven heat to 275°F (140°C) and bake for 20 minutes. Turn over and bake another 20 minutes.

MAKES 3 DOZEN BISCOTTI.

Meringues

A low-fat snack for sweet cravings!

3 egg whites	Beat until stiff, but not dry.
1 cup (250 mL) granulated sugar	Add very gradually to eggs. Beat for 10 minutes, or until very thick.
¾ cup (175 mL) shredded coconut ¼ cup (50 mL) chopped pecans (optional) ¼ tsp (1 mL) vanilla	Combine and fold into beaten egg whites.
	Drop spoonfuls of the mixture onto waxed-paper-covered cookie sheet. Bake at 350°F (180°C) for 25–30 minutes, or until lightly golden. MAKES 3 DOZEN.

Raspberry Coulis

Serve as a sauce for ice milk, yogurt, and other fruits.

2 cups (500 mL) fresh or frozen raspberries ¼ cup (50 mL) granulated sugar	Combine berries and sugar in saucepan. Simmer over low heat for 2 minutes, or until raspberries are softened. Stir constantly to prevent burning.
2 tsp (10 mL) cornstarch 2 tbsp (25 mL) cold water	Dissolve cornstarch in water. Add to berries and stir for about 30 seconds, or until fruit is translucent. Strain through a fine sieve, pressing to extract as much pulp as possible. Cool.
	MAKES 1½ CUPS (375 mL) OF COULIS.

Peach Shortcake

A hearty dessert with little fat and lots of summer flavour. I adapted this recipe from a much richer recipe with sour cream. Everyone actually likes this one better!

1½ cups (375 mL) all-purpose flour 1 tbsp (15 mL) baking powder 1 tsp (5 mL) baking soda	Sift together dry ingredients.
½ cup (125 mL) brown sugar Pinch salt	Add to flour mixture.
⅓ cup (75 mL) shortening	Cut into flour mixture.
1 egg, beaten ¾ cup (175 mL) 2% milk	Combine eggs and milk and add to flour mixture, which will become a stiff batter.
½ cup (125 mL) chopped pecans (optional)	Add to batter. Bake in 9-inch (23 cm) round pan at 375°F (190°C) for 25 minutes. Cool, then cut horizontally. Set aside to cool.
2 cups (500 mL) plain low-fat yogurt ⅓–½ cup (75–125 mL) brown sugar	Mix together yogurt and sugar. Set aside.
4 cups (1 L) peeled, pitted, and sliced peaches	Place one layer of cake on plate. Spread with yogurt mixture and top with peaches. Add second layer of cake, another layer of yogurt mixture, and top with peaches.
	Serves 8.

Pavlova

Attractive, delicious, and nutritious.

3 egg whites	Beat eggs until stiff, but not dry.
⅔ cup (150 mL) granulated sugar	Gradually add sugar to egg whites and beat for 10 minutes, or until thick.
½ tsp (2 mL) vanilla	Fold into egg whites. Cut 10 circles out of parchment paper. Arrange on cookie sheet and cover each circle with egg mixture. Shape into cups using back of spoon. Bake at 275°F (140°C) for 25 minutes or until lightly golden. Set aside to cool.
2 cups (500 mL) yogurt or frozen yogurt, any flavour	Fill meringue cups with yogurt.
2 cups (500 mL) chopped strawberries, blueberries, raspberries, kiwi, banana, etc.	Top yogurt with fresh fruit.
	SERVES 10.

Amaretti

This recipe makes cookies that are chewy at first—then become crispy if they last a couple of days. Both work!

1 cup (250 mL) ground almonds 1 cup (250 mL) granulated sugar 2 egg whites	Beat with electric mixer for 3 minutes. Let stand for 5 minutes.
24 blanched almonds	Spoon mixture gently into piping bag with 1/2-inch (1 cm) plain tube. Pipe onto cookie sheet (that has been sprayed with cooking spray) in a circular motion from centre out. Place cookies 2 inches (5 cm) apart. Place an almond on top of each cookie. Bake at 350°F (180°C) about 12 minutes or until light brown.
	MAKES 24 AMARETTI COOKIES.

Pistachio Bread
(a thin crisp cookie)

These are a welcome addition to any dessert table as they are low in fat and very satisfying. The thinner you cut them, the more you can eat! If you do not have a 9- x 5-inch (2L) loaf pan, use an 8- x 4-inch (1.5L) pan instead, cutting the cookies into 24.

3 egg whites ⅓ cup (75 mL) granulated sugar	Beat with mixer until soft peaks form. Gradually add sugar beating until it's dissolved between additions.
¾ cup (175 mL) all-purpose flour ¾ cup (175 mL) shelled pistachio nuts 1 tsp (5 mL) finely grated orange rind ¼ tsp (1 mL) ground cardamom	Fold all ingredients into egg-sugar mixture and pour into a 9- x 5-inch (2 L) loaf pan sprayed with cooking spray and lined with parchment paper, extending 1 inch (2.5 cm) above long side of pan. Bake at 350°F (180°C) 30 minutes until light brown. Cool in pan, remove, then wrap in foil and let stand overnight. With a serrated knife, cut into very thin slices, 1/4 inch (1 mL) or less. Place slices on ungreased baking sheet and bake in a 250°F (120°C) oven 15 minutes until crisp. MAKES 24 COOKIES.

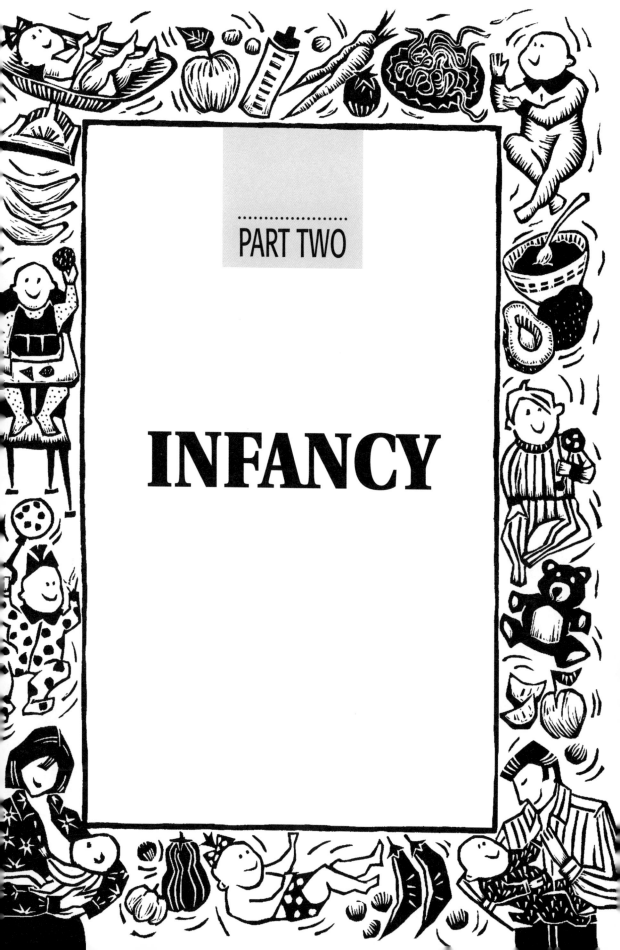

PART TWO

INFANCY

T HE FIRST YEAR OF LIFE IS A REMARKABLE TIME FOR parents as well as the new member of the human race. Your newborn arrives with little more than the capacity to be fed, but by the time her first birthday is celebrated, she can manipulate a wide range of foods— as well as people. This section provides the information you need to think about even before the baby arrives. Whether you choose to breast-feed or bottle feed, this chapter will answer some of your questions. We also discuss introducing baby's first foods and the delight of finger foods. There are guidelines to follow and suggestions on how to manage the whole food adventure. In addition, we have provided some creative recipes to tempt the most discerning young gourmets.

It's a Baby!

When your baby arrives, you will be so absorbed in the challenges of parenting that you won't have much time for decision making. The time to think about how you want to feed your baby is when you are still pregnant. The first decision has to do with breast-feeding vs. bottle feeding. Later, you will have to make other decisions about family eating patterns and the role food plays in the life of your child. Most of these decisions will depend on the attitudes to food you have developed through personal experiences.

People who grow up with healthy attitudes towards food and body image will pass this gift on to their children by their own example and by their response to their children's eating patterns. People who grow up with fears about food and body image may recreate these harmful attitudes and behaviours in their children. If they perceive themselves as overweight, they may restrict their child's food intake, or deny them certain foods they consider to be fattening. There are a few examples in the pediatric journals about mothers with a history of anorexia who underfeed their children, causing growth retardation. On the other hand, parents with childhood memories of others teasing them for being skinny or small may try to overfeed their children to encourage growth. In either case, parents run the risk of creating unnecessary food issues with their kids. If you have had difficulties with eating disorders or body image yourself, it might be harder for you to pass on a healthy attitude towards eating to your children. We hope this book will provide some guidelines, but you might want to consider visiting a counsellor or dietitian to overcome these difficulties and to ensure that you are receiving ongoing nutritional advice.

Whatever your early experiences may have been, you need to understand the different effects that food can have on your child's growth, development, and behaviour. You will probably find yourself discussing your questions in great detail with other new parents and with doctors, friends, and relatives. These include questions about the most basic infant feeding and caring issues, from breast-feeding to diapers and from sleeping arrangements to the latest infant music recordings. The purpose of this chapter is to give parents an understanding of the feeding issues relevant to the first year of life. The next chapter will focus on feeding children who can feed themselves.

Breast-Feeding vs. Bottle Feeding

The human race has survived because of breast milk. Although breast-feeding is a natural, healthy way to feed your child, there are now a few generations that have been successfully fed by formulas based on milk. Until safe formulas were available, breast milk was the only reliable way to feed new babies and ensure their survival. In earlier times, wet nurses were chosen to feed babies for mothers who were unable or unwilling to breast-feed. These substitute breast-feeders were women who had recently had their own babies or women who had never stopped producing breast milk after their last baby was born. The selection of the wet nurse was often based on the woman's personal qualities, because people believed that human characteristics were passed on through the breast milk and that a wise woman could pass her wisdom on to the new child.

Today, with all of the effective formulas on the market, there is not much call for wet nurses. If a mother is unable or unwilling to breast-feed, she can opt for one of the many formulas now available and be assured that her child will thrive.

During the 1960s, the "return to nature" movement set the stage for a resurgence in breast-feeding, to counteract the move to so-called "scientific" infant feeding that began in the 1950s. At that time, the popular notion was that scientists could outdo Mother Nature. During the 1970s, political activism and a spate of deaths of bottle-fed babies in the less-developed countries created a new emphasis on the importance of breast-feeding. Television, magazines, and books reinforced the virtues of breast-feeding. Health care professionals joined the bandwagon and before long, breast-feeding became the norm. As a result, the number of breast-feeding mothers in most of the higher-income nations rose consistently and reached a peak in 1984, but for some curious reason, has been gradually falling ever since.

In parts of Canada, the numbers have remained quite high relative to other parts of the world. However, many advocates of breast-feeding are wondering what might account for the decline of breast-feeding in countries such as the United States, Britain, and Australia. One explanation may be related to some of the problems women experience in their efforts to breast-feed. Even though members of every other species manage to feed their babies without trained instructors, humans simply are not born with this knowledge. Nor do women in industrialized countries regularly see others breast-feeding successfully, which would help them mimic the behaviour. During her hospital stay, a new mother needs clear information as well as reassurance and support to help her feed her baby properly. In Canada, all health professionals are called upon to support and promote breast-feeding where appropriate.

With hospital stays growing ever shorter, your access to a nursing instructor will be limited and any problems that develop at home will require someone else with knowledge and a supportive attitude. Your obstetrician is mainly interested in the delivery and anything related to its success or failure. Your pediatrician is mainly interested in the baby. Unless you are seeing a woman doctor who has also breast-fed, your family physician may not be intimately familiar with breast-feeding problems. What you need is ready access to a professional, friend, or relative with the experience, knowledge, and time to help you through the first few weeks. A good book on breast-feeding is also essential to help answer your questions. Your local public-health office is also available to provide advice and support.

There are many advantages to breast-feeding that outweigh some of the problems. Breast-feeding reduces the chances that babies will suffer from allergic reactions, since babies are seldom allergic to their mother's milk. Breast milk is very convenient and economical. It requires no preparation or sterilization, and is always ready to serve. The only cost is the extra food required to feed the mother so that she has the energy demanded for milk production. Some of this energy comes from the extra fat that is naturally stored during pregnancy for this purpose. Many women might see this as a real advantage: eat more and lose weight at the same time! There are also a number of irreplaceable ingredients in breast milk. These include the mother's antibodies, which offer protection against illness during the first few months, as well as hormones and certain fats that encourage healthy growth and development. Even though scientists have been able to identify and measure most of these components, the only way of giving all of them to babies is through the cheapest food on the market: breast milk.

Researchers have also investigated the role of breast-feeding in terms of the protection it may offer women against cancer and osteoporosis in later life. It may protect babies against ear infection, respiratory disease, and diabetes. Breast-feeding is also an important recommendation for reducing obesity in later life. This feeding method allows babies to establish their own appetite control mechanisms. As mothers cannot see what is consumed, the baby is the expert on how much is enough.

Women need to know about some of the problems they may encounter with breast-feeding. These include engorged breasts, cracked nipples, and infections inside the breast tissue. Infections require medical intervention, but most women are advised to continue breast-feeding. As for the other problems, you can continue to breast-feed with knowledge, support, and help. Women may also switch to bottle feeding because they are worried that the baby isn't getting enough sustenance, because they find breast-feeding too exhausting, or because there is no one else to feed the baby when they are not available. As long as the baby continues to grow and has six to eight wet diapers per day, you can have some assurance that the baby is getting enough milk.

Although both breast-fed and bottle-fed babies grow well in length, weight, and head circumference in the first six months, recent evidence suggests that formula-fed babies grow faster. This has sparked great debates about the merits of bottle feeding, and formula companies promote this information whenever possible. But there is a key question that has not yet been answered to anyone's satisfaction: is faster growth advantageous or harmful in the long run?

Ultimately, the decision to breast-feed or bottle feed is a personal one and no woman should be made to feel that she has made an error in judgement. Your key concern should be to learn the proper techniques of infant feeding, whatever method you choose.

Breast-Feeding

You should start breast-feeding as soon as possible after your baby is born. Although your baby has practised sucking and swallowing even before delivery, you need to learn how to provide milk. This may require some instruction and practise.

During the first few days of life, mature milk has not yet formed. Instead, the baby receives colostrum, a thin yellowish liquid loaded with antibodies and nutrients that protect the baby during the first days of life. Between the second and fifth day after delivery, your breasts will suddenly feel quite full and may hurt because of the production of mature milk taking place at this time.

A fascinating aspect of breast-feeding is that the production of milk responds directly to the baby's demands. The more the baby

suckles, the more milk is produced. If only all our demands were so easily accommodated! This is why it is important to continue to breast-feed your infant on a regular basis to ensure that milk production develops into an established pattern. This principle also supports the decision to breast-feed on demand. For most mothers and for their babies, it is easier to feed when the baby appears to be hungry. However, this can be a difficult call, because babies cry for a variety of reasons; hunger is not the only one. They may cry because they want comfort, warmth, or a change of diaper, or simply because they are feeling fussy. They may also cry if they need burping. This sort of cry may accompany the strange behaviour of pulling away from the bottle or breast even while they are trying to feed. (Babies need regular burping, regardless of the type of feeding selected.) It is amazing how quickly most mothers learn to distinguish the cry for food from other sounds.

Setting up a feeding pattern takes at least the first few weeks of life and may take as long as three months. Most babies will settle into a feeding pattern of about every two and a half to three hours in six weeks or so. As your baby nurses, your breasts will respond by producing milk. Gradually you will both adjust, but just when you think you have figured out a workable routine, things begin to change. Perhaps it is a return to work or other responsibilities that require some adaptation. Whatever the reason, you'll find yourself making continual adjustments from now on.

Breast milk provides almost all of the nutrients a baby requires. One notable exception is vitamin D. In the Canadian climate, and with our efforts to protect ourselves and our babies against the rays of the sun, babies require vitamin D supplements daily. Be sure to consult your baby's doctor to discuss the appropriate amount as the recommendations vary for different geographic areas.

Feeding the Nursing Mother

Nutrition is just as important when you are breast-feeding as it is when you are pregnant. In fact, now you really are eating for two and your nutritional requirements are even higher than they were during pregnancy. Good nutrition will ensure that you produce adequate milk and that you protect your own body stores throughout this time. To meet your own needs and those of your baby, you should make every effort to get nourishing food, plenty of rest, and emotional support. Relaxed and healthy mothers provide the best start for happy, healthy babies.

Breast-fed babies have fewer digestive problems, but many women blame themselves for any problems their babies have during nursing, such as diarrhea, gas, rashes, or fever. You shouldn't have to eliminate any of the food groups from your own diet to combat any of the baby's feeding problems. However some women are advised to stop eating vegetables in order to reduce gas. Other women may be advised not to drink milk or eat cheese to reduce colic in the baby. Unless there is a very good reason for eliminating a particular food, such as a known familial allergy to specific foods like nuts or peanuts, this approach could cause nutritional problems for you later on.

For example, restricting dairy products during nursing may cause problems when you are older. This is because it takes a lot of calcium to make breast milk. If your diet does not provide calcium, a supplement would be in order. This situation is aggravated if the time between weaning one baby and starting another pregnancy is short. Frequent pregnancies, with long periods of breast-feeding, place such a high demand on the mother for calcium that unless you are getting plenty of calcium and vitamin D in your diet, your bones will be the source of the baby's calcium.

At present, nutrient supplements are not routinely recommended for nursing mothers unless there is a specific reason. Teenagers and strict vegetarians may need them, as well as women who have to avoid dairy products because of lactose intolerance or women who have special dietary restrictions.

Almost any variety of food in the diet will give you the energy you need for milk production. However, the nutrients in your diet must be high enough to supply your milk with nutrients and spare your body stores. Therefore, the use of a vitamin-mineral supplement during this period of time should be considered in the same way as during pregnancy.

The food you eat will not strongly affect the nutrient levels in your milk but instead will affect the flavour and composition of the milk. For example, the level of fatty acids in the milk will reflect the mother's own intake and may also reflect her own body fat if she is losing weight. If she eats lots of butter, beef, and cheese, her milk will be higher in saturated fats. If she eats mainly vegetable oils, grains, and cereals, her milk will be higher in unsaturated fats. Dairy farmers have known about this effect for years!

If you are breast-feeding your baby, you will produce about 30–35 fluid oz (850 mL–1 L) of milk a day, which costs an extra 1,000 calories a day. Your need for energy is now higher than it was when you were pregnant. Some of the extra calories may be provided by the fat that your body stored during pregnancy. During breast-feeding, you may lose a pound (0.45 kg) a week, or you may find that your weight does not begin to drop until after you have finished breast-feeding, because the increased volume of breast tissue keeps your body weight a little higher than normal. Throughout this time you should continue to eat to appetite.

As much as a quart (1 L) of fluid is lost each day through the breast milk. To supply the fluid for milk, you'll need plenty of water and other liquids. Have water, juice, or milk on hand at all times.

All mothers may need extra iron if they lost a lot of blood during delivery. It may be necessary to take a supplement until your body stores have recovered. As long as you are not menstruating, your need for iron will return to the level before pregnancy. Although breast-feeding may stop menstruation for several months, this is not a signal to stop using birth control.

Special Concerns

Breast-feeding and exercise

During the first three months after the baby has arrived, you may feel an exhaustion that cannot be explained by lack of sleep alone. Fatigue may be partly the result of the continuous production of milk, which demands a lot of energy from your body. For this reason, you should set reasonable goals for yourself so that you don't overextend your resources. You need to recover from childbirth, to care for your newborn, and to support breast-feeding.

Within a few weeks or months, depending on your lifestyle, you may be keen to return to some sort of exercise. Studies have not shown any major effect of exercise on milk volume or composition. However, after a heavy workout, your milk will contain higher levels of lactic acid, possibly giving it a sour taste. If your baby does not nurse well after you have been exercising, consider reducing the intensity of exercise or give the baby formula for the first feeding after a workout. You and your baby may be more comfortable if you nurse before exercise. That way you can enjoy the exercise and the baby can enjoy the meal.

Combining breast-feeding and bottle feeding

The decision to breast-feed doesn't mean that you will never use a bottle. You may need more than two hours off once in a while. If you plan to use bottles occasionally, introduce one before the baby reaches four to six weeks. This will ensure that he will accept one in an emergency situation. If the mother requires a regular time away from the baby, give him a bottle at approximately the same time each day. This will help your milk production to be lower at that time and it will give other members of your family a chance to feed the baby.

If you wish, a daily routine bottle may be introduced at around 5:00 p.m., when you may feel most run down. In the event of extreme stress or exhaustion, your milk production may diminish and both you and your baby will benefit from a planned bottle. Keep in mind that the baby may not accept a bottle from you because he prefers breast milk, so it's helpful to have someone else available to provide the bottle. Or, you might replace the 2:00 a.m. feeding so that the baby's father can participate at that time and give you the additional sleep you so desperately need during this period.

Even though introducing a bottle at the same time each day will ultimately cause the breast to reduce milk production at that particular time, milk production will be just as good at the other feedings of the day. This is because of the stimulus of the baby's suckling and the production of milk, which responds to it.

Feeding other fluids to your baby

During the warmer months, babies may occasionally be thirsty and require water between regular feedings. Tap water is safe to use and should be boiled for at least two minutes before it is cooled completely for the baby to drink. This sterilization process should be used until the baby is four months old. Bottled water from natural underground springs can be used but it typically has no fluoride. Look for bottled waters specifically labeled for babies and do not use mineral water or carbonated soda water. Limit any use of fruit juices as they provide calories that may displace the more nutritious calories that come from breast milk or formula. Babies should never be fed herbal teas or other herbal beverages as they may contain harmful natural ingredients. Nursing mothers should also avoid drinking large amounts of these teas as any harmful compounds may be passed on through their breast milk. Use water only to satisfy your baby's thirst; do not use bottles of water in lieu of a pacifier or feeding.

Occasionally your baby may have some mild or moderate dehydration associated with diarrhea or vomiting. When this occurs, speak with your physician; you may be advised to use an oral electrolyte solution (OES) along with the usual feeding routine (breast milk or formula). This feeding pattern is also known as ORT (oral rehydration therapy). The OES contains specific concentrations of carbohydrates, sodium, potassium, and chlorides to promote fluid and electrolyte absorption and to speed up rehydration. Other drinks such as teas, juice, or sport drinks do not have these compounds in the same proportions.

Returning to work

If you are planning to return to work, you may continue to breast-feed or you may wish to introduce a bottle. While you are away from the baby, you will need to replace the daytime feedings one by one with feedings of formula or expressed milk. Gradually, over the course of a four-week period, you can cut back on your milk production during the hours that you will be at work. When you are at work, the baby can have a bottle and when you're at home, she can breast-feed. What you do on the weekends will depend on your body's reaction to this routine. You may be able to breast-feed all day Saturday and Sunday and produce adequate milk without experiencing any problems on Monday when you return to work. Or you may have a very low milk supply and find yourself with a very hungry baby on the weekend. It's possible that on Monday, after the daytime stimulation of breast-feeding on Saturday and Sunday, your breasts may feel engorged and may even leak. It's just a matter of experimenting to decide the best strategy for meeting your particular needs. The best advice is to test out each situation and decide what works best for you.

You may want to continue to breast-feed exclusively even when you are back at work. Exclusive breast-feeding is recommended for the first six months of life. This means pumping milk at the usual time of feeding in order to continue the normal routine. You can use a manual breast pump, an electric breast pump, or hand manipulation. Store the milk in a refrigerator at work. Label it carefully! The milk should be used within the next 24 hours or should be frozen. If you find it difficult to pump milk from the breast by hand, an electric breast pump can be a very effective way of extracting milk quickly. Electric pumps are expensive to buy, but you can rent one from a hospital or from a company that specializes in renting medical equipment. Pumping allows your baby to get the benefits of breast milk during the first six to twelve months, even when you have returned to your former routine.

When to wean the baby from breast-feeding

The decision to wean the baby from breast-feeding is a highly personal one. It may also be culturally determined. In some areas breast-feeding for longer than a year is encouraged because of the poor food supply. In highly developed countries, where extreme poverty is not a problem, the issues are different. The benefits of breast milk are most important during the first six months of life. After babies have begun to consume a wide range of foods, the nutritional benefits of breast milk continue to make a contribution to growth, development, and nutritional status.

Bottle Feeding

One of the main concerns with feeding your baby formula is the preparation of the formula and maintaining the highest possible level of sanitation. Different types of formula have different methods of preparation and different shelf lives. Read each label carefully. Certain formulas are ready to serve and require no added water. They are easy to use but often expensive. Liquid concentrates require you to add water; if you give your baby the undiluted form, it could damage the baby's immature kidneys. Powdered formula is often the cheapest, but it should not be used for longer than four weeks after it has been opened. For a casual user of formula, this is wasteful. The type you choose will depend on your budget and on the frequency with which you plan to use formula.

You may find it convenient to prepare only one bottle at a time. Sterilize all the measuring and feeding instruments carefully before use. Wash your hands too. Add sterilized water to the liquid or powder (depending on the formula) and warm it for your baby. Don't use a microwave oven to warm the baby's bottle, because it will heat the liquid unevenly, leaving hot spots in the milk that can cause burns. You can keep formula bottles for one day in the refrigerator before you use them, but an unfinished bottle should be discarded immediately. If your baby has an allergic reaction to formula, try a soy formula but be sure to talk to your pediatrician about any allergic reactions.

Don't try to make your own formula to save money. Homemade formulas do not provide the correct balance of nutrients that babies need. If you're considering bottle feeding, you must be prepared to accept the expense and responsibility of selecting the proper formula. Iron-fortified formulas are recommended.

The timing of bottle feeding is different from that of breast-feeding. You cannot let your baby drink from one large bottle in fits and starts throughout the day. Although this technique resembles the "on demand" schedule of the young breast-fed baby, it is unsafe to leave the formula at room temperature for more than two hours. A schedule of small (2–3 oz/50–75 mL) bottle feedings in the first few weeks will help establish a rhythm. During each feeding, pay careful attention to regular burping.

When babies are bottle fed, it is easy to see how much they have consumed. You may overfeed your baby if you encourage her to finish the bottle. Try to be fully attuned to your baby's appetite. This includes recognizing when she is hungry and when she is full, and responding appropriately. While feeding on a schedule is easier to do with a bottle, feeding on demand is more natural and will allow the baby to regulate her own appetite. Overfeeding in early life could set the stage for poor appetite regulation (i.e., obesity) in later life.

Fussing and Feeding

It is not unusual for babies to fuss or cry between feedings. They may be quite happy to have something in the mouth even when they aren't hungry. Don't use water as a substitute for a pacifier or milk. A small infant drinking more than 8 oz (225 mL) of water at a feeding is at risk of water intoxication. Pacifiers are important to some infants because their need to suckle often exceeds their need for food. Without a pacifier, they may cry excessively for oral gratification. The pacifier will provide this without overfeeding the baby. Although some have noted that the use of pacifiers may diminish the baby's breast milk intake. Without a pacifier, most will eventually find a thumb or finger to suck. When the time comes, it is easier to wean them from the pacifier than from a thumb.

Over the course of the first few weeks, you may discover that your child has a specific time of day when she is especially fussy. After the first few months, your baby will develop a more regular routine of feeding and napping. Until this happens, however, there may be a fair bit of confusion. The duration of periods of crying and fussing seems to increase up until about six weeks and then decreases. Many infants cry during the evening hours and often into the late evening. Others may be fussiest from 4:00 a.m. to 7:00 a.m. or from 9:00 a.m. to 11:00 a.m. If your baby cries continuously and pulls up her legs with large volumes of gas, she has colic. If you are breast-feeding, your doctor might consider a change in your own diet. For formula-fed babies, a change in formula may be helpful. Babies differ widely when it comes to crying and fussing behaviours. Some families find the first few months very exciting (with the possible exception of those middle-of-the-night feedings!). For other families, those months are sheer torture, as the baby cries constantly. Endless days turn into sleepless nights and the stress level rises dangerously. Although this time seems like an eternity, either of these patterns will pass as the baby matures beyond the first several months. What each family needs is patience, perseverance, and some perspective. Some may require significant help from family, friends, or professionals. Just remind yourself that one day this child will actually take off with friends and ignore you!

Giving Vitamin and Mineral Supplements to Babies

The Canadian Paediatric Nutrition Committee has indicated that babies do not need nutrient supplementation from six to twelve months if they are getting formula fortified with iron and eating other foods that contain iron and vitamin C. The only supplement that is recommended is vitamin D for the breast-fed infant. Breast-fed babies whose mothers are strict vegetarians will also need vitamin B_{12}.

Many parents do not realize that bottled water does not contain sufficient fluoride to prevent dental caries (cavities). Discuss fluoride with your baby's doctor. Fluoride is not recommended for babies less than six months but may be recommended for six- to twelve-month-olds when they use a water supply that is not fluoridated (e.g., well water or bottled water with less than 0.3 ppm fluoride).

Most infants are given a vitamin K injection or drops immediately after birth because they are born without their own supply. Vitamin K helps to clot blood. In adults, vitamin K is produced by intestinal bacteria. A good dietary source is green leafy vegetables, but we don't rely on these when the bacteria are doing their job. Newborns have been in a sterile environment, however, and have no bacteria in their intestines at first. In order to make sure that they do not develop a bleeding problem after delivery (hemorrhagic disease of the newborn), hospitals give them vitamin K right after birth. After the first few days, they no longer need an injection unless they are placed on antibiotics, which wipe out those helpful bacteria.

Babies also need iron in their diets. A low level of iron in young children can cause learning and behaviour problems. This awareness of the importance of iron is reflected in feeding recommendations for babies that promote the use of iron-fortified formulas for formula-fed babies for the first year of life. Babies who receive breast milk get iron in a form that is quickly absorbed, so they do not need iron supplements until they begin solid foods.

Introducing Solids

The decision to introduce solids is not always a simple one. At one time it was fashionable to give babies cereal as early as possible. Parents were rather competitive about their baby's diets and often boasted about the wide range of foods their babies would eat at a very early age. Nowadays we recognize that introducing foods too early is unwise. Babies cannot digest cereals until they are at least three months old. They will swallow them, but they get no nutrients from them. Eating cereals at too early an age may also mean that the baby is drinking less breast milk or formula. The early introduction to certain foods may set the stage for allergic reactions later on.

How can you tell when your baby is ready for solids? In general, the best indicators come from the infant. One sign babies give is that they are no longer satisfied with breast milk or formula alone. They might show this by continuing to cry for more after the bottle or breast is empty, or by waking up hungry in the middle of the night to eat after weeks of sleeping through the night. Another sign might be a slowing down of growth. You will find this out at the baby's routine health checkups when his weight and length are measured. This slowing down would suggest he needs extra calories from solid foods. A baby demonstrating interest in food eaten by other family members can sometimes also be an indication. Remember, however, that for the first six months, breast milk or formula can provide the baby with the most complete and nutritious food. In fact, this is the only time in our lives when a single food will do the job. After the signs of readiness for solids are confirmed, a new set of feeding practises needs to be introduced.

Dramatic changes take place from the sixth to the twelfth month of life. Babies go from a state of complete reliance on one food provided by others to feeding themselves a diet similar to that of the rest of the family. Throughout this period, keep feeding your baby either breast milk or iron-fortified formula. He should continue to receive as much breast milk, or formula as he wants along with his solids. Since mothers cannot tell how much breast milk their babies are getting, breast-fed babies can continue to control their own intake. Gradually introduce food from all four food groups until the baby is eating a variety of healthy foods at the end of twelve months.

Do not give your baby regular milk before he is one year old—because it does not contain iron and it can irritate the stomach. However, if cow's milk must be used, make sure it is whole milk and not 2 percent or skim milk. This recommendation holds until your baby is two years old; it will ensure that he gets enough fat and not too many salts. Some parents take nutritional advice intended for adults and apply it to their babies. They do not realize the importance of fat in a baby's diet. Fat is needed for a baby's growth and development, especially for brain cells and nerve tissue.

The Canadian Paediatric Nutrition Committee recommends that the first weaning food for infants be iron-fortified cereal. This gives babies a good source of iron to coincide with the increased need for iron, which occurs at four to six months of age. Introduce new foods one at a time and repeat them the next day, with a minimum three-day wait before you try an additional new item. This method will help to determine whether the baby has any allergic reaction to a particular food. Foods that are most likely to cause allergies, such as strawberries, peanuts, egg whites, or seafood, should not be introduced until after one year. If there is a family history of allergy to particular foods, then those foods should be introduced much later.

The first time you give your baby cereal, he may have trouble getting it into his mouth. Prepare for a messy encounter and enjoy the ride. You can thin out the cereal with liberal amounts of breast milk or formula to make it easier for him to swallow. Once he can get the food from the spoon into his mouth, add less fluid to make a thicker mixture. Later, the cereal can be lumpy and you can add fruits for a more interesting flavour and texture. Gradually he will get used to the changing textures and learn how to handle these in his mouth. It takes time to develop chewing and swallowing skills.

Patience and a positive attitude will go a long way in helping you and your baby to enjoy this new experience.

Start by giving your baby one to two tablespoons (15–25 mL) of cereal twice a day. Once he accepts the cereal, you can increase the volume of the feedings and time them to coincide with family meals. For example, within a month of getting him started on cereal, you can feed your baby six tablespoons (100 mL) of cereal with three ounces (75 mL) of milk, either breast milk or formula, at approximately 7:00 a.m., 11:00 a.m., 4:00 p.m., or 7:00 p.m. Over time, you can adjust each of these "meals" to resemble breakfast, lunch, snack, and dinner. As you add new foods, the feedings will reflect the family's usual meal choices. Between meals, feed him breast milk or formula. As the meals become larger and more varied, your baby will need less and less milk between meals and snacks. After about twelve months he may eat only the meals and snacks, with milk as a starter for the day and at bedtime.

The recipe section for this chapter has a full range of food preparation instructions, including full dinners for baby.

Pay attention to the timing of meals and the amount of food you provide. When you introduce new foods, the baby should have a good appetite for them. It helps when he isn't too hungry or too full. Try feeding him milk from one breast or giving him the first half of a bottle, then introduce the new food, followed by breast-feeding from the other breast or from the remainder of the bottle. An alternative is to start with solids as between-breast-feeding "snacks."

Put a small amount of the baby's food on the end of the spoon and put the spoon towards the back of the baby's mouth. This will counter the extrusion reflex, which makes a baby spit out food with his tongue. This is not necessary with an older baby, who will quickly learn to move the food back himself.

Never put cereal or mashed food in a bottle, because this may cause choking.

After cereal has been mastered, vegetables or fruits can be added gradually. They provide vitamin C as well as other important vitamins and minerals. A high intake of orange or dark green vegetables such as cooked carrots, peas, winter squash, or other foods high in beta carotene may cause hypercarotenemia, a high blood level of carotene that may temporarily turn the baby's skin orange. This is quite harmless and disappears when the foods are reduced. Foods to avoid during the weaning period are home-prepared spinach, turnips, carrot soup, and carrot juice, which can cause another blood problem (methemoglobinemia). This is because of the nitrites in these products. The nitrite levels rise when these foods are stored in the refrigerator for one or more days. For variety, use green beans, well-cooked cauliflower, and summer squashes (which are not as high in beta carotene).

Some fruits and vegetables can be eaten raw. Banana, papaya, and avocado are ideal because of their mushy texture. Don't be alarmed by the brown fibres they leave behind in your baby's diaper.

The last food group to be added is the meat group; this includes meat, eggs, fish, and cheese. Canned fish, mashed without the bones, is a good source of protein. Other protein-rich foods include yogurt, peas, well-cooked beans, and lentils, which provide protein sources similar to meat products. In the meantime, add pasta, rice, mashed potatoes, breads, and other starchy foods to form a more complete meal.

You may find it relaxing to prepare and feed the baby his food before the family meal when you have the extra time and attention needed for the job. Make sure everything you use is clean.

At six to nine months of age, your baby can accept naturally soft foods, which can be mashed and introduced without a great deal of preparation. These include banana, avocado, papaya, applesauce, and well-cooked vegetables. Cooked meat, fruits, and vegetables should be crushed through a sieve to make them the right texture for young babies to swallow and digest. Food processors or baby food grinders are ideal at this time. In addition, you can use commercially prepared infant foods, which are manufactured in factories under the highest possible standards of cleanliness. These foods are convenient and well tolerated by infants. However, they may be somewhat expensive. Check the prices for yourself.

Foods for your baby can be frozen in small meal-sized batches and reheated as needed. If you reheat them in the microwave, be sure to stir them carefully to distribute the heat. Remember that the microwave oven can create hot spots in food that can burn your baby's mouth.

The weaning diet should be based on a diet of breast milk or formula with the gradual addition of foods that are typical of your family's food. Eventually, all four food groups will give the baby the nutrients and energy necessary to meet her requirements for growth and development.

Finger Foods and Self-Feeding

As soon as your baby can transfer an object from her hand to her mouth, you can give her hard bagels or teething biscuits to support the skill required for self-feeding. This skill often appears when a baby is teething, and these foods can provide some comfort to her gums. Do not use foods that break up easily in the mouth because they can cause choking (e.g., crackers, rolls, regular biscuits).

From eight to twelve months, babies develop the pincer reflex, which allows them to pick up small food pieces between thumb and forefinger. Some people call this the "Cheerio stage." You can prepare small pieces of cereal, meat, fruit, and vegetable and the baby can feed himself at last. During this time you can add an increasing variety of food to his diet, such as pieces of toast or grilled cheese sandwiches.

During the first year, do not give your child honey because it is known to contain the spores of the organism that causes botulism. Children under three should not be given foods that could cause choking or aspiration, such as whole nuts, large peas or beans, popcorn, grapes, or large berries. Other foods to avoid are hot dogs cut up into slices that would block the throat, or foods that form balls in the mouth, such as peanut butter sandwiches. Keep sweets to a minimum because they cause tooth decay and because they take up space that should be used for more nutritious foods. As soon as your baby's teeth erupt, they are vulnerable to dental decay. Brush or wipe your baby's teeth clean with a cloth or soft toothbrush after meals and before bed. And never put a baby to bed with a bottle. The sugar in the fruit juice, milk, or sweetened drink will cause cavities if the liquid stays in the baby's mouth

overnight. Two ways of avoiding this problem are to encourage the use of a drinking cup as soon as your baby can manage one and to clean her teeth before bedtime.

By 12–18 months of age, your baby can consume most of the food that the other members of your family eat. Your main goal at this time is to encourage her to enjoy a variety of foods and to develop some independence in feeding. With patience, persuasion, and perseverance you'll enjoy the stages of feeding your child successfully and welcome her at the family dinner table as a regular member.

How Much Food Do Babies Need?

Some babies are far more active than others and need more food; others are passive or slow growers and need fewer calories. These differences are based on a combination of genetic predisposition and individual characteristics. The general health of a baby will also affect her appetite. When a baby is ill, her appetite may decrease. This is often the first sign of a cold or flu. When she feels better, her appetite returns and her growth catches up. Feed your child to meet her particular appetite. Do not force-feed her, but try to ensure that she gets enough calories to keep her healthy. Of course, this can be easier said than done. I've encouraged my children to take just one more bite only to have them throw up on the plate after eating beyond their appetite. You really shouldn't mess with Mother Nature.

The Second Year

During a child's second year, the rapid growth that was typical of the first year begins to slow down. You may notice that your child is less hungry and less interested in food. It is important to recognize that it is growth that drives appetite, not the other way around. Forcing babies to eat will not make them grow any faster, but may teach them to hate food, or to overeat.

You may, however, find that your child has become more curious about food and may seek out food by sampling things around the house. Desires for pet food, ice, or other strange requests may be signs of an iron deficiency.

During this time, children enjoy finger foods, which are easily handled, such as cut-up fruits and vegetables, crackers, cheese slices, and dry pieces of cereal. Give your child small amounts at a time to ensure that she is not overwhelmed by large amounts or prone to overeat, and to minimize the mess. Your child may insist on feeding herself and should not be rushed. If this causes problems with the rest of the family, start her mealtime early, so that she gets a head start. Allow her all the time she needs to eat in peace. If she is eating cereal, give her a glass of milk to go along with it to make the most of the cereal's nutritional value. This is an important time when children develop skills and new pride in their abilities to feed themselves.

Snacks

It is important to plan snacks so that they contribute good nutrition to the overall diet. Snacks can include cheese and crackers, vegetables and dip, cut-up fruits, or cereal. Like mealtime, snack time requires a comfortable setting and parental supervision to ensure safety. Avoid foods that cause choking and don't let your toddler walk, play, or run around with food in his mouth. The car is not a safe place for children to snack unless you are in the back seat with them on a long trip together. As children get older, they may be tempted to play games by catching tossed food in their mouths. This can also lead to choking.

During the second year, your child needs whole milk, not skim milk. However, 2 percent milk may be advisable in certain cases such as obesity. Discuss this concern with the baby's doctor. Eggs and previously avoided foods such as seafood can be introduced at this time. Some children want specific foods such as eggs or peanut butter sandwiches every day. My first son liked tuna sandwiches so much that he had them for breakfast! Now, he won't even take them to school for lunch. It is not unusual for children to go on food jags. Don't worry about this unless it lasts for many months.

The most disconcerting part about feeding the child between ages one and two comes when his growth starts to slow down and his appetite plummets. This is normal. As long as you provide healthy foods you know he enjoys, your child will eat well and thrive.

INFANCY

RECIPES

INTRODUCING SOLIDS TO YOUR BABY IS AN EXCITING NEW STAGE. Follow the order recommended by your baby's doctor and you will be surprised by the fun you'll have trying new foods. When I was making Mira's baby food, I used very simple guidelines. Following Rena's expert advice, I found the process to be not only challenging, but indeed great fun! I hope you will agree.

First Vegetables

Carrots

Scrub and peel 2 bunches fresh carrots, slice on diagonal.

To make in microwave, place carrots in pyrex dish, add 3–4 tbsp (50–75 mL) water, cover, and cook on High for 5–6 minutes. Check to make sure they are very tender. To make in steamer, cover and steam over boiling water 7–10 minutes.

Put carrots in blender or processor. Purée until consistency is a soft mush. Add a little boiling water until the consistency that you want has been achieved. Spoon into ice cube trays. Cover and freeze. Put cubes into plastic bags, remove air. Date and label the bags and return to freezer for up to 1 month. Thaw and use within 2 days. When serving the carrots, remove one frozen cube at a time. Leave at room temperature to defrost, then place in a baby food warming dish until warm enough to serve.

When first introducing vegetables, make sure that they are very soft and mushy. As the baby gets older, more texture can be added. If you are using the microwave, be very careful to defrost evenly. Test the food to make sure that it is evenly warmed.

Frozen Peas

Place 2½ cups (625 mL) frozen peas in 4 tbsp (60 mL) water in microwave, covered, and cook on High for 4 minutes. Purée in blender or food processor until desired consistency. Freeze and label as recommended for carrots. To steam, place peas in steamer, cover, and simmer over boiling water 6–8 minutes until tender. Makes one ice cube tray.

Sweet Potatoes and Yams

Peel and cut 3 medium sweet potatoes or yams into 1- x 2-inch (2 x 5 cm) cubes. Microwave, covered, on High 7–8 minutes until tender and soft. Purée according to instructions for carrots. Or steam over boiling water 12–15 minutes until tender. Purée and freeze as usual. Makes one ice cube tray.

Winter Squashes

Acorn, squash, butternut, hubbard—all are sweet and delicious. Scrub outside and cut 1 butternut or hubbard squash or 2 acorn squash into large chunks. Microwave, covered, on High for 5 minutes. Turn around and microwave additional 4–5 minutes until squash is soft. Scrape squash from skin. Purée in blender or food processor with a little water until desired consistency is reached. Or steam, covered, over 2 inches (5 cm) boiling water 18–20 minutes until soft. Spoon into ice cube trays and freeze according to instructions for carrots. Makes two ice cube trays.

First Fruits

Applesauce

Wash, peel, core, and seed 6–8 apples. Cut into large chunks. Place in bowl, cover. Place in microwave 2–3 minutes on High until soft. Purée in blender. Fill ice cube trays and freeze. Remove from trays. Place in plastic freezer bags, remove air, date, and label.

Bananas

Mash ¼ ripe banana very well with a fork. Add ½ tsp (2 mL) breast milk or formula. Make sure that the banana is very soft and mashed completely. Give small portions to the baby.

Avocados

Mash ¼ ripe avocado very well with a fork. Ripe avocados should mash very easily with a fork. Overripe avocados have an unpleasant taste that your baby will not like.

Papayas

Mash ⅛ ripe papaya very well with a fork.

Mangoes

Mash a few tablespoons and serve to baby.

Peaches

Peel, pit, and slice 3–4 peaches or nectarines. Place in bowl and cover. Microwave 1–2 minutes on High until very soft. Purée in blender or food processor and freeze. Peaches should be cooked initially. A few months later they can be introduced raw.

Foods for Babies Eight Months or Older

Vegetables

Wash and peel 4–5 small white turnips or 1 yellow turnip. Cut into small chunks. Steam for 4–6 minutes in a microwave in small amount of water until soft. Purée in blender or food processor with 1 tbsp (15 mL) apple juice. Spoon into ice cube trays, cover, and freeze. Transfer to bag, remove air, label, and date.

Other vegetables suitable for eight-month-old babies include broccoli, asparagus, and zucchini. Prepare using same method as for turnips.

Last introduction of vegetables

Use 12 oz (340 g) package frozen white baby corn kernels. Place in bowl and cover. Microwave 6–7 minutes on High until very soft. Purée in blender with a little water, breast milk, or formula. Freeze in ice cube trays, covered. Place in bags, remove air, date, and label.

Introduce beets and brussels sprouts cooked in this manner and peeled and seeded raw cucumber.

Fruits

Cantaloupe, honeydew melon, grapes (peeled and mashed).

Introducing meats

Mama Rozzie's Chicken Soup

Purée some cooked chicken with broth to a smooth consistency. Pour into ice cube trays, cover, and freeze. Transfer cubes to freezer bag. Remove air and label, date, and freeze. This should be the first meat introduced to your baby.

Dinners for Baby

New foods should be introduced one at a time. Once the baby has been fed a new food over the course of three to four days and had no adverse reaction, the new food can be blended with others to make complete dinners.

General directions for complete baby dinners

1. Simmer together all of the ingredients in a saucepan on medium heat for 20 minutes.

2. Pour all of the mixture into a food processor, blend, and serve.

3. Leftovers will not freeze well if they contain potato; other dinners will freeze well. Do not save foods that have been left over on the feeding dish.

4. Initially the mixture should be very smooth. Add more water if necessary to get a smoother texture. As baby gets older, less water and blending are necessary.

Veal Scallopini Dinner

3 oz (90 g) veal
$^1/_2$ cup (125 mL) carrots, fresh or frozen
1 small potato, peeled and diced
$^1/_2$ cup (125 mL) water

Harvest Chicken Dinner

1 boneless chicken breast
$^1/_2$ cup (125 mL) cooked rice
$^1/_2$ cup (125 mL) winter squash, peeled and diced
$^1/_2$ cup (125 mL) water or chicken broth

Maritime Dinner

3 oz (90 g) boneless and skinless halibut or salmon
1 small boiled potato
$^1/_4$ cup (50 mL) peas, fresh or frozen
$^1/_3$ cup (75 mL) water

Asian Chicken

1 small boneless chicken breast
$^1/_2$ cup (125 mL) rice noodles
$^1/_2$ cup (125 mL) peas
Dash low-sodium soy sauce (optional)
$^1/_2$ cup (125 mL) water or chicken broth

Spaghetti à l'enfant*

$^1/_2$ cup (125 mL) cooked pasta, any shape
3 oz (90 g) ground veal cooked in $^1/_2$ cup (125 mL) tomato sauce

follow steps 2–4 only (from page 156)

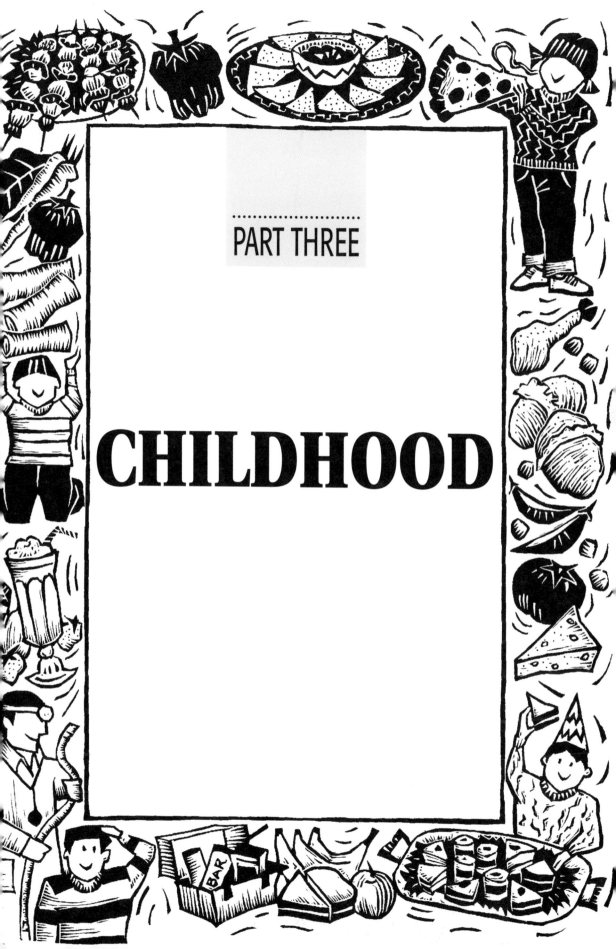

PART THREE

CHILDHOOD

THE NUTRITION RECOMMENDATIONS FOR CANADIANS are designed to reduce some of the chronic diseases known to be linked with diet. These include obesity, cardiovascular disease, and cancer. These recommendations are primarily intended for the adult population, even though they claim to be intended for anyone over the age of two. They include maintaining a healthy weight; reducing total dietary fat; increasing complex carbohydrates (starch and fibre); and limiting sugar, salt, caffeine, and alcohol. However, there are no guarantees that following the perfect diet (even if such a thing exists) will prevent you or your children from getting a chronic disease.

The application of these recommendations to young children should be accompanied by an understanding of their unique needs. Overzealous calorie and fat restriction can interfere with children's growth and development. The information in this chapter should help parents to understand their children's nutritional needs.

The practical application of the nutrition recommendations for Canadians is *Canada's Food Guide to Healthy Eating*. In the second half of this section, we will show you how to apply *Canada's Food Guide to Healthy Eating* to planning your children's menus. There are simple, reliable, kid-tested recipes that combine good nutrition with good eating. Note that the recipes are not intended for children with special dietary problems such as allergies, lactose intolerance, diabetes, and so forth. Consultation with a dietitian as well as a local organization dedicated to each of these problems is recommended.

Choosing Healthy Diets

Your goal as a parent, when it comes to feeding your children, is to ensure that they grow to be strong and healthy. You can help them develop a positive attitude towards eating a variety of interesting and nutritious foods. Start by accepting that they have a certain body shape, which may not be the average shape. Some parents fret over their child's height (too short, too tall) and others over their weight (too thin, too fat). Much of the worry is rooted in their own experiences of childhood, particularly if they themselves were ridiculed because of their size or shape. These parents may become overanxious about their children's eating habits, hoping somehow to influence their growth and development.

We hope the information in this section will help parents overcome these concerns and enable them to form more positive attitudes towards food and eating. They'll not only help their children, but themselves as well.

Many parents believe that childhood eating habits will persist throughout adulthood. Some are terrified by the prospect that their children will eat nothing but chicken fingers and peanut butter sandwiches for the next 80 years. But think back to what you ate as a child. Now think about the foods you have learned to enjoy since then. Most adults learn to appreciate a wider variety of foods as they grow up and chances are that your kids will want a more interesting menu one day.

Another myth about children and food that has been around for many years is that children have an inborn ability to select a balanced diet. In the 1920s, a researcher by the name of Dr. Clara Davis studied very young children and their ability to select a nutritious diet. She provided them with a wide range of healthy foods and demonstrated that they did, in fact, choose foods from all four food groups. However, only the most nutritious foods were available. The children were offered fruits, vegetables, meats, cereals, and milk. There were no cakes, candies, or soda pop to choose from. Their willingness to select a good diet from the foods available was really a test of their curiosity and not their nutritional wisdom. However, the experiment did show that children naturally prefer variety in their diets as opposed to monotony. Unfortunately, this research was misinterpreted by others who believed that children would choose a healthy diet if left to their own devices. This is only true when children are offered exclusively healthy choices and no so-called junk food.

In our society we have a wide range of food choices, including cookies, chips, candy, and pop, just to mention a few examples. Try to think of these foods as "sometimes foods." They will not do your child any harm when they are a small part of an otherwise well-balanced diet. But they do take up space that could be used for more nutritious foods. And for some children there may be a limit to the space they are willing to fill. Think of the foods that are high in vitamins, minerals, and other nutrients as "everyday food." These are the ones that make up the four food groups. You may need to do a little promotion on these foods to compete with the heavily advertised "sometimes foods." These labels might help to remove the notion of "good" and "bad" foods. The biggest danger in using the "good food" and "bad food" labels is that we begin to label ourselves when we eat them. How often have you said, "I was bad today," when you are talking about eating so-called "bad foods"? How often have people told you that they have been "good," when they were really talking about what they ate? Must we measure our personal worth by the foods we eat? Are we setting the stage for eating disorders in our children when we impose this sort of baggage on them?

There are no such things as bad foods, only bad diets. Take, for example, a chocolate bar, which is high in sugar and fat and low in nutrients. As part of a diet made up of a balance of the food groups, the chocolate bar can add energy to the total daily intake, provided that the energy is spent. However, if you eat that chocolate bar with a can of soda pop as lunch after a morning without breakfast, then it represents a major portion of the day's intake and is a poor food choice. It is the context in which we choose a single food that is important, not the food itself.

In order to ensure that your children consume a wide variety of highly nutritious foods, it's up to you to set good examples through your own eating habits. Nothing is more damaging to parents' credibility than to insist that their children eat fruits and vegetables while they eat chips and candy. I have also seen parents tell their children that they cannot have dessert and then sit down to their own heaping serving of pie or cake. Parents can be most helpful to their children when they try to establish a positive attitude towards trying new foods, consume a healthy diet, and keep food in perspective. Be prepared to practise what you preach.

You can ensure that your children get all the nutrients they need from food (rather than from supplements) as long as you provide them with adequate servings from each of the four food groups.

Most of us learned about these groups in our early school years and have used them as a mental checklist from time to time ever since. The Canadian food guide recommends that children have two servings of meat or meat alternatives each day. *Canada's Food Guide to Healthy Eating* was designed for children over four with the following recommendations. We have added our own suggestions for children under four.

Recommended Serving Sizes		
	4 and older	**under 4**
Meat & Alternates 2–3 servings/day	2–4 oz (60–125 g) meat $^1/_3$ cup (75 mL) beans, tofu 2 tbsp (25 mL) peanut butter	2 oz (60 g) meat 2 tbsp (25 mL) beans, tofu 1 tbsp (15 mL) peanut butter
Milk 2–3 servings/day	1 cup (250 mL) milk 2 oz (60 g) cheese	$^1/_2$ cup (125 mL) milk 1 oz (30 g) cheese
Fruits and Vegetables 5–10 servings/day	1 fruit $^1/_2$ cup (125 mL) vegetables	$^1/_2$ fruit $^1/_4$ cup (50 mL) vegetables
Breads & Cereals 5–12 servings/day	1 oz (30 g) cereal $^1/_2$ cup (125 mL) pasta or rice 1 slice bread	$^1/_2$ oz (15 g) cereal $^1/_4$ cup (50 mL) pasta or rice $^1/_2$ slice bread

These are recommended serving sizes and are not meant to be a rigid prescription. The number of servings and amounts will vary for each child according to his appetite. Remember that health, growth, and activity all influence appetite from day to day. In addition to these food groups, you can add various oils such as soy, canola, or olive oil to ensure that they get sufficient essential fatty acids.

These guidelines consider foods as the raw materials for meals and recipes. Naturally, families from different heritages will combine them in very different ways to create unique meals. They are still an excellent tool for parents and others responsible for children's diets to use when assessing whether there are any foods missing from the child's diet on a day-to-day basis. You can use them not only in meal and snack planning but also for shopping or selecting from a restaurant menu.

Unfortunately, there can be a downside to pushing your children to eat a good diet. When you become overly concerned about whether your children are eating the more nutritious foods, such as meats or vegetables, you often send them mixed messages. Typically parents bribe children to eat healthy foods by rewarding them with less healthy choices. For example, we tell children that turnips are good for them and if they eat them, they will be rewarded with ice cream. Children quickly figure out that if they have to be rewarded for eating their vegetables, then vegetables must not taste very good. Similarly, they realize that a food used for reward tastes good and is probably bad for them. As a result, children start to assume that healthy foods taste bad and that good-tasting foods are unhealthy. An alternative is to make the majority of the offerings healthy and allow the child some choice. Parents have a responsibility to provide a variety of healthy foods for their children but it is up to each child to determine how much to consume of the various options.

Remember, your children may not share your taste in food for a number of reasons. Children are more sensitive than adults to food temperature. If a child burns her mouth on a specific food such as soup or a cheese omelette, she may retain a negative association with that food that goes beyond her exact memory of the event. As a result she will avoid that food for a long time before trying it again. Children have more taste buds than adults and therefore are more sensitive to stronger flavours in foods. This explains why some children have a natural dislike for certain foods with strong flavours, such as vegetables or meats. As a general rule, they prefer sweet and mild flavours. Children are also more resistant to certain textures than adults. Most of them dislike the slimy texture of foods such as cooked asparagus, spinach, or mushrooms, and prefer crisp and crunchy foods such as crackers or raw carrots. Eventually, most children come to accept a wider variety of foods as a result of changes in perception or as a result of the repeated introduction of these foods. Researchers have found that in order for a child to become familiar with a food or even to be willing to try a food, you may have to present it as many as 10–15 times!

Obviously it requires enormous patience and persistence to get children to eat certain vegetables, and, frankly, it may not be necessary. Instead of fighting over spinach as a source of folic acid and beta carotene, offer them orange juice or carrots. Orange juice is loaded with folic acid and vitamin C, and a few carrot sticks provide plenty of beta carotene. Keep in mind that the food group includes both fruits and vegetables. There is no harm in focusing on the fruits while giving children the small number of vegetables they actually like to eat. Remember what you ate as a child. Over the course of time, you came to enjoy broccoli, eggplant, and mushrooms. Instead of fighting over vegetables, consider other strategies to ensure that your children get a complete diet. Keep in mind their natural preferences for mild, sweet, crispy, and crunchy foods. Put raw vegetables in a salad or serve them with their favourite dressing as a dip. Hide them in soups and sandwiches. Disguise them in spaghetti sauce or in sandwiches. Ask your children to help you plan the family's menus. Then sit back and pray for success.

Meal Patterns

When families routinely eat dinner together, the benefits to children are tremendous. Parents who hope to stay sane while coping with work, child care, and other responsibilities want to avoid the "restaurant syndrome" at mealtimes. That's what happens when each person in the family chooses different foods for dinner. The alternative is making one family meal for all adults and children of different ages. This could unfortunately translate into meals that represent the lowest common denominator. In other words, to avoid conflict, the parents end up eating only those foods the children are willing to eat. This gets very boring and turns mealtimes into chores instead of pleasant experiences. There is a huge personal incentive for parents to encourage children to eat a wide range of interesting recipes.

Children are influenced, not only by their parents, but also by other children. You can take advantage of this situation to expand your child's eating habits. Often a child will try a new food in the presence of a friend or when he is away from home. This is one of those times we are happy to see children succumb to peer pressure. It is always worthwhile to ask children when they return from summer camp, day care, or a school trip whether they discovered any new foods. If the answer is yes, it may be possible to add something new to the family eating pattern. One summer, my kids came home from camp asking for tacos and submarine sandwiches. Of course, no system is completely foolproof. I'll never forget the boy who begged his mother for Spam after enjoying it on a canoe trip only to spit it out when she finally served it! Some foods lose their appeal when eaten out of context.

Another opportunity to outsmart the opposition is to introduce new foods to children when they have friends visiting. Your chances are even better when you have a known "good eater" as a guest. In the presence of their friends, your children may try new foods that they wouldn't touch with only the family around the table.

Even after children have become accustomed to a varied and healthy diet, it pays to sustain their interest with appropriate meal routines. Children need both physical and emotional comfort at mealtimes to ensure a healthy appetite. Seat very small children at a low table or on a booster seat with utensils that are small enough for them to use independently. Make sure that they have plenty of

time and no deadlines to meet. The amount of food on the plate should match their capacity to eat it, so that they are not overwhelmed by the task. A room that is free of distractions such as toys, television, and other activities will allow them to concentrate on the food. Even a table piled with magazines and books will provide sufficient distraction to keep them from eating. When the radio plays their favourite song, don't be surprised if they leave the table to imitate the latest rock video. Above all, let them respond to their own appetite and don't force them to clean their plates.

Emotional comfort is just as important at mealtime as physical comfort and desirable food. Meals can be a time for friendly family discussions or fierce confrontation. The cues will generally come from the adults in charge. It's hard to eat when people are discussing upsetting or revolting subjects. The mention of a dirty diaper or worms in food can bring an abrupt stop to an otherwise pleasant experience. Sibling bickering can have the same effect. Set the mood for eating just as you set the table.

Although many North American families have settled into a pattern of a small breakfast, small lunch, and large dinner, this pattern does not work for everyone. One child may be able to eat a large breakfast and lunch but arrive for dinner with a very small appetite. Others are not hungry at all in the morning but can eat well by the evening.

Research suggests that it is best to eat most of our calories in the earlier part of the day. In any case, know the natural appetite pattern for each child and work with it rather than against it. If your child's appetite peaks do not coincide with the usual pattern, plan meals to provide samples from all food groups when she is hungry. Serve full-course meals for breakfast or lunch with lighter fare for dinner, if that will ensure a good day's nutrition. Plan snacks carefully so that they complement meals (see page 173).

Breakfast

Children and teenagers may want to skip breakfast. Studies show that breakfast skippers are unlikely to make up the missed nutrients during the rest of the day. In general about 25 percent of the day's total energy should come from breakfast. Because of the foods we most often include, breakfast provides us with an important set of nutrients. That is because we generally include a fruit, giving us a stable source of vitamin C, grains (such as rice and bread) or cereals (hot or cold) providing healthy fibre, carbohydrates, and milk, which provides protein, calcium, and vitamin D. Your child may not get these foods at other meals. Without breakfast, a child could fall short of the daily needs for each of those nutrients.

The reason for skipping breakfast may be related to the breakfast habits of the parents (as many as 18 percent of adults have only coffee or tea for breakfast) or to the fact that both parents may be working and children are left to prepare their own breakfast. Given the choice of sleeping late, watching television, or preparing their own breakfast, most children will opt to skip breakfast. Another reason children skip breakfast is their personal concern about weight. All the evidence about weight maintenance indicates that eating breakfast is essential to keeping a healthy weight. Most of the calories that are missed when breakfast is skipped are made up during the rest of the day, but the nutrients are not. Skipping breakfast does not help anyone to lose weight and may actually increase the risk of obesity.

When children skip breakfast, they often have more difficulty performing tasks at school. They may have trouble concentrating because blood glucose, the only source of energy for the brain, has run down since their last meal 12–15 hours before. Without that source of energy, many experience nausea and fatigue and have consistently poor performance on standard achievement tests. Teachers can often identify the children who have not had breakfast because of their apathetic or irritable attitude during the morning. For this reason, many school districts have introduced breakfast programs to ensure that children who don't eat breakfast at home do get breakfast at school. These programs have been evaluated and they provide proof that breakfast can enhance children's behaviour and learning.

It is easy to get kids to eat cereal in the mornings. It does not much matter which cereal you pick. There are some on the market that are made of whole grains, but almost every breakfast cereal is fortified with a similar level of nutrients. If your children like the sweetened cereals and refuse the whole grain ones, don't argue. Just make sure they brush their teeth afterwards. It is not worth fighting with children to get them to eat breakfast when they are getting what they need from their favourite cereal. It's also helpful to remember that many outgrow their preference for the sweeter cereals or get bored with them eventually. However, one option is to mix together one sweetened and one unsweetened, higher-fibre cereal.

Protein at the breakfast meal helps keep energy levels high throughout the morning by helping sustain blood glucose levels for several hours. Eggs and milk are not the only sources of protein you can have for breakfast. Consider peanut butter, tuna, cheese, or other meat alternatives. Our granola recipes (pages 45 and 213) and pancakes are also worth trying.

Snacks

Like mealtimes, snacks can become a source of conflict for children and parents. Unlike adults, very young children need snacks between meals to ensure that they get an adequate intake of the food groups. Until they are six, children will benefit from a mid-morning snack as well as an afternoon one. This routine has been built into many school kindergarten programs. Once children reach the first grade, there is no particular reason to provide most of them with snacks to eat during school hours. They should be using recess time for activity instead. Unfortunately, there has been so much promotion of children's snack foods that some school yards look like garbage dumps at the end of the recess period.

For kids who need a snack, after school is an ideal time. These snacks can provide a good opportunity to encourage young children to eat fruits, vegetables, and nutrient-dense foods (such as milk, cheese, and rolls) that they might not eat at meals. One way of ensuring this is to present children with a variety of attractive and healthy snacks after school and in the evening. If your cupboards are full of chips, candies, and other "sometimes foods," don't blame your children for eating them. Instead, plan and prepare snacks for children when they get home from school. These could include a fruit platter, vegetables and fresh yogurt dip, oatmeal cookies, and milk. We have some great snack recipes at the end of this section. Most children will not go to the trouble of taking fruit out of the refrigerator, washing it, and cutting it up, but they will gladly eat fruit if it is presented to them when they are hungry.

A planned snack time also prevents the problem of the

revolving kitchen door and the tracking of food all over the house. Even more important, the timing of snacks can also keep children from spoiling their appetite for meals. Provide snacks at least one and a half to two hours before meals so that your child's appetite can recover in time for dinner. In fact, some children find it easier to eat a well-balanced dinner when they are moderately hungry rather than "ravenous." Very young children cannot recognize that they are hungry and may express their hunger in cranky behaviour, which can derail a well-planned meal.

School Lunches

Parents often complain about the monotony of preparing school lunches. It's not just the task that becomes monotonous, but the foods themselves. It is not unusual for children to request the same sandwich every single day!

Our suggestions have three purposes. First, all of us (especially kids) are concerned about the environment and schools are trying to encourage litter-free lunches. So we will focus on foods that can be packed with a minimum of waste. Second, the meals must be nutritious; *Canada's Food Guide to Healthy Eating* is, as always, a good tool for planning these meals. Third, children must like the food. This prevents waste and ensures that they don't trade away your masterpieces for something that is below your high standards.

Sandwiches are convenient to prepare, pack, and eat. Draw up a list of sandwiches each child is willing to eat so that when you find yourself in a rut, you can refer to this list. You can often get kids

to eat vegetables by including them in sandwiches. Add lettuce and tomato to a turkey sandwich and you have a "sub." To make sure that you have a fresh (not a soggy) sub, pack the lettuce and tomato in a plastic container and let your child put the sandwich together at school. Other vegetables that make sandwiches more interesting are alfalfa sprouts and thinly sliced cucumbers. Make sure that you thoroughly wash any sprouts. Use a separate container to keep it all fresh. If you add mayonnaise to sandwich fillings, spread the fillings on frozen bread to keep the sandwich cold longer. Another way to keep sandwiches cool is to freeze the drink you include. As the drink thaws during the morning, the food stays cold. Try some of the exciting party sandwiches at the end of the recipe section. They can be made ahead and frozen. Add fruit for dessert or fruit juice in your own container. Encourage your school to sell milk at lunch time for those who would like milk because this food will not keep well through the morning in a lunch bag.

One worthwhile investment is a thermal food jar. You can send soups, stews, or pasta dishes in them. This provides a great change from sandwiches and the food really stays warm. It works especially well if you fill the jar with hot water as you prepare the food. Dump the water, add the lunch, and you will be amazed at how warm the food stays during the day. In fact, even leftovers come home warm!

Try sending our Split Pea and Barley Soup (page 225) or macaroni and cheese as a main course. You can also send leftover pastas or quesadillas. Round out the meal with cut up vegetables and fruit.

Once children have access to their own money, they have new-found freedom to buy foods that you might not have in your house. A few basic principles are worth keeping in mind. First, children need to learn how to make purchasing decisions at some point. They need to learn that money can be saved for something special as well as spent impulsively on an attractive candy or toy. Buying chocolate bars or chips on their way to or from school can be an expensive routine and will wipe out their wallets (as long as you don't simply give them more money).

Second, the snacks they buy may simply add extra calories to their intake and may not ruin their appetite for meals. As long as they are growing well and brushing their teeth regularly, there is unlikely to be any problem. A worse problem is created when they are led to believe that these foods are somehow very special or very bad and they become secretive about eating them. Finally, children should feel secure knowing that all the food they really need is provided at home and that they do not have to use their own money to feed themselves.

Growth, Development, and Appetite

To find out whether your children are growing and gaining weight adequately, take them for regular medical checkups. You shouldn't need to weigh and measure your children at home. In fact, I think home weigh scales should be abolished! They create unnecessary anxiety and fear.

Normally, children will have growth spurts during specific stages in their lives. The most common times are during the preschool period between the ages of four and six and again during the preadolescent period between the ages of 10 and 13. During these times it is common for children's appetites to increase. Remember that the stimulus for appetite comes from the growth itself and not the other way around. You cannot make a child grow more or faster by feeding him extra food.

Children should continue to eat to their own appetites as they did when they were infants. When children keep in touch with their appetites and with the signals from their bodies that tell them when they are hungry and when they are full, they will avoid the dangers brought on by an early preoccupation with weight. Children should never be forced to eat; nor should food be withheld from them when they are truly hungry. Food should be used to provide nourishment and not as an activity or as a reward. Otherwise children may learn to use foods to escape from boredom or to reward themselves for non-energy-spending activities. Although food offers us great pleasure and should be an enjoyable experience, the regular use of food as an escape from boredom or as a reward can set the stage for obesity or other eating disorders in later years.

It is possible to spoil children's appetites for good food. Giving a child a snack just before a meal will cause a change in appetite. Research has shown that high-carbohydrate food, such as fruit, bread, or crackers before meals will decrease total intake and may lead children to eat more protein. One might take advantage of this theory and try giving children a small carbohydrate snack before dinner to encourage their consumption of meat. On the other hand, eating a protein snack such as cheese, milk, or sliced meats before a meal will make the child favour carbohydrates as the major calorie source during the meal.

In addition to foods that spoil the appetite, children may lose their appetite if they are overtired. Let the children have some quiet time after an active day at school, even if this means letting them flop in front of the television for half an hour before dinner. This is a good opportunity for them to unwind from the physical, mental, and social activities of the day and build up their appetite for dinner.

Other appetite spoilers are distractions, such as the desire to rush from the table to see a favourite television program. Activities planned for immediately after dinner such as sports, games, or special events can also put a damper on eating. Arguing or teasing each other at the table can also spoil appetites. Unfortunately, children often recover their appetites soon after the kitchen has been cleaned and may grab cookies, candies, or cakes to fill the void. The policy in our household is that "the kitchen is closed" after it has been cleaned. To protect parents from that revolving kitchen door with kids eating continuously between meals, the emphasis on good eating behaviour needs to be supported with appropriate time, place, and food selection to ensure that children get adequate nutrition at mealtimes.

Healthy Weights

Growth in height and weight is a normal part of childhood. Unfortunately, our society has become phobic about weight gain in adults and this has been transmitted to young children who have also become preoccupied with their weight. Girls may begin to worry about it as early as five or six years of age, and their concern may be related to the effect of television as much as to the influence of parents and other role models who are preoccupied with their own weight.

A survey in the United States of children between grades 3 and 6 demonstrated an extraordinary obsession with weight and thinness. Of the group of children studied, 45 percent said that they wanted to be thinner and 37 percent said they had already tried to lose weight. Six percent of the children under the age of 13 were eating so little that they were close to the condition of anorexia nervosa. A survey of adolescents revealed even higher proportions. Seventy percent of teenagers said that they were fat and 37 percent were dieting at the time of survey.

Children as young as five show a desire to avoid obesity and soon after the age of five begin to understand the relationship between eating and obesity. Children have been known to restrict their diets to the point at which they have actually stopped growing. If this happens, they may not achieve their normally expected height. In order to prevent this kind of behaviour, parents should have a healthy attitude about their own weight. Once they have achieved this, they will be able to impart to their children a healthy attitude towards growth and development. This is not an easy task when 70 percent of Canadian women indicated in a recent survey that they are trying to lose weight—even when they are well within the range of healthy weights.

Genetics plays an important role in determining body shape and composition. Whenever I am in a mall or a park where families are walking together, I am always impressed by the similarities in the size and shape of parents and their children. Part of the story is the way the family eats, but recently it has become clear that genetics is a major factor. Studies of identical twins raised apart show that they are more likely to resemble each other in weight than their adopted siblings. Surveys also show that if one parent is obese, then a child has a 50 percent chance of being obese. If both parents are obese, the chances for the child are 80 percent. Parents concerned about the genetic potential they pass on to their children need to first come to terms with their own weight and then develop a positive strategy to ensure that their children develop healthy eating and activity patterns.

In addition to providing good nutrition, demonstrate your support for healthy physical activities. Your whole family can enjoy activities such as walking, biking, swimming, or sports together. Participation is important for the development of positive health behaviours and positive attitudes towards our bodies. All members of the family should be encouraged to participate in daily physical activities, especially ones that develop skills that can be carried on through adulthood. Sports such as tennis, skiing, or soccer are energy-demanding sports that are lots of fun for children and are easy to pursue through adult life. Noncompetitive forms of dance, figure skating, and swimming can also be healthy activities. Encouraging a good variety of physical activities from an early age enhances physical and skeletal development and coordination, and encourages children to develop self-esteem and a positive self-image, as well as good sporting attitudes and control over their bodies and their emotions. Ideally, each child will find one or more activities to provide excitement and pleasure for a lifetime.

In addition to family involvement, we need to lobby for strong physical education programs in the schools. These should provide children not only fitness and fun but a sense of discipline and the knowledge of how to care for their bodies, improve muscle strength, enhance flexibility, and maintain physical activities to promote cardiovascular fitness. Strength, flexibility, and cardiovascular fitness are all components of physical well-being and need to be nurtured by the family from the very beginning and sustained through the school system and the community.

Avoiding Obesity

Over the past decade, rates of obesity in Canada have tripled for adults as well as for children. While genetics can explain some of the obesity that develops in children, the rapid increase can only be attributed to a change in lifestyle. When children develop obesity, it is especially difficult for them to be active as they are physically uncomfortable and may be embarrassed to do sports. Their weight issues are likely to continue into adolescence and adulthood setting the stage for diseases such as diabetes, cardiovascular disease, and even some cancers. Therefore preventing obesity is the best option for families and is quickly becoming a priority for health advocates and politicians. Some useful strategies for parents are provided in this section and should be combined with advice from the previous section "Healthy Weights." However, it is important to use the family physician to diagnose any weight issues so that you avoid any excessive focus on your child's weight.

A positive approach to balancing energy includes a kitchen with ample amounts of healthy foods for meals and snacks. Avoid stocking up on "treats" for a special occasion as these will only serve as a constant source of conflict. Buying bulk quantities of cookies, candy, and desserts may appear to be cost effective but these will displace healthy foods and lead to over consumption. If you offer your child a choice of apple, orange, or banana, they will choose a fruit.

It is important for all of us to learn to regulate our own food intake. Those who are natural regulators are "in touch" with our body's signals of hunger and satiety, and typically do not experience unhealthy weight fluctuations. Those who are unable to respond effectively to hunger and satiety signals are at risk of poor weight regulation and may develop obesity or other food-related problems such as disordered eating. To promote healthy appetites, plan regular meals and use snack time to add fruits, vegetables, or milk to your overall diet. Eat at a table in the kitchen or dining room with plenty of time to enjoy food and conversation. Meals that start with soup, salad, or vegetables and dip will slow down the pace of eating and help us to stop eating when we have had enough to eat. Encourage water consumption to get fluids at mealtimes without extra calories and avoid the use of sweetened beverages at all times. Do not eat food in front of the television as this minimizes our awareness of hunger and satiety and may promote overeating. Homes that have combined kitchen and family rooms may promote unhealthy family eating patterns and should be carefully managed.

Eating out has become more routine than ever and fast food restaurants are an easy and inexpensive family option. Encourage children to make good choices and to avoid the "super sizes." Research has demonstrated that we eat more food when we are given larger servings. With so much attention given to obesity these days, the fast food chains have been developing healthier options. Vegetarian pizza with whole wheat crust can be a healthy and tasty option. The salads and plain grilled meats are also healthy choices. It may be useful to discuss the options before you arrive and if you are interested, you can now get nutrition information from each chain's Web site. Soon this information will be available in each franchise.

Just as children need a variety of healthy foods, they need a variety of healthy activities. Television, computers, and video games should be limited to one hour per day. Young children should have a play room that allows for healthy indoor activity including balls, climbing apparatus, and music to encourage dance and motion. Regular walking is also important and children should be encouraged to walk to school. If parents are concerned about safety, organize a "walking school bus" in your neighbourhood so that working parents can ensure their kids routinely walk to school. Most can arrange to arrive later on one day per week and employers should be supportive of such a program. If children have a long commute that requires a bus or car, they should be dropped off a few blocks away to get some routine exercise.

When they are old enough, encourage them to participate in a variety of organized sports that emphasize participation and skill development. Participation once a week is not sufficient and should be combined with an active daily routine, including biking, skating, or skateboarding. When out and about, encourage the use of stairs instead of escalators and park a distance from the stores to increase your time for walking. Children can also be active around the house with chores such as shoveling, yard work, or helping with groceries, cleaning, and laundry. Regular physical activity and healthy eating can prevent obesity in childhood and set the stage for a healthy lifestyle throughout adulthood as well.

Sugar

Animals of all kinds have a very strong preference for sweetness. In fact, when animals are given sugar, they will reduce their intake of food to increase their consumption of sugar. This is probably because sugar is something that we like from the moment we try it. In fact, it may even be related to the role that sugar has played in our earliest history and our survival. Sweet foods are a quick and easy source of energy. Athletes know this, and so did our earliest ancestors.

Is there any harm in sugar? Many have connected "overdoses" of sugar to a range of problems, from hyperactivity, obesity, and cardiovascular disease to criminal behaviour. There is no compelling research to support these claims. However, excessive consumption of sugar can cause dental caries, particularly when the sugar is consumed steadily. For example, all-day suckers or hard candies that are kept in the mouth for a long time foster the growth of the micro-organisms that are the true guilty parties when it comes to dental caries. The micro-organisms use sugar for their own energy and in doing so create an acid that destroys the enamel of teeth. This allows them to invade the teeth and cause further damage. In order to break the cycle we need to eliminate the source of energy for these bacteria, and the best way of doing that is to brush the teeth after meals and snacks that contain sugar. If tooth brushing is not possible, then certain foods will help clean the teeth. Apples, celery, and other abrasive foods will clear away the sticky sugar and prevent the bacteria from using it.

Foods that are sticky and remain in the teeth also promote the development of the bacteria. These include dried fruits, such as raisins or prunes, as well as peanut butter and jelly sandwiches, which provide hours of energy for the micro-organisms. Therefore, careful food selection as well as oral hygiene can help to reduce the number of dental caries from the time teeth first erupt.

Fortunately for many North American children, fluoride has been added to our municipal water supply and this enables them to develop teeth that are more resistant to decay. Bottled water, however, does not contain comparable levels of fluoride. Nevertheless, you should keep an eye on your children's consumption of sugar products.

Sugar has been implicated in obesity. However, the true impact of sugar on obesity is hard to assess. Research on the diets of obese children compared to those of average-weight children suggests that their diets are not dramatically higher in calories. An important difference between the two groups tends to be the amount of activity in their daily routine. Overweight children are less active than average or underweight ones. Their sedentary habits develop after they gain weight, thus creating a vicious cycle of increased intake, reduced activity, and weight gain. Encouraging children to enjoy activity and discouraging recreational eating are two positive ways to prevent obesity. And from all the best reports to date, it is clear that prevention is better than treatment.

Finally, sugar has been linked in the popular press with hyperactivity in children. It is interesting to note that under experimental conditions, sugar consumption is associated with increased serotonin in the brain. Serotonin is a neurotransmitter (brain messenger) that induces sleep. Researchers have shown that a high sugar intake makes subjects feel sleepy. Research with children who are given sugar has shown that there is no effect on hyperactivity whatsoever. Nevertheless, parents and teachers will claim that when candies are brought into the classroom there is a change in the children's behaviour. This may be more of a social than a physical phenomenon, given the excitement associated with special days and sweet food. Children may feel especially excited to be getting such foods at school or at a birthday party and may react with unusual behaviour. Is it the sugar or the context in which the food is provided?

I once planned a birthday party for fourteen nine-year-old boys. They played baseball for an hour and then ate cake, ice cream, and chocolate milk. When the parents arrived to retrieve them, they were surprised to find even the most active boys sitting quietly in the backyard. Why? During the last ten minutes of the party I gave out the party favours; each boy got two packs of baseball cards and they were all busy studying their loot and negotiating trades. All the sugar and chocolate caused no reaction at all and the active baseball game helped them to relax.

Humans do not have a nutritional need for sugar; it is not an essential requirement. We like sugar and we can use it to enhance the food that we eat. There does not appear to be anything dangerous about consuming a reasonable amount of sugar in foods. Children can eat a certain amount of sweets if they get an adequate amount of all the necessary nutrients in a day and still need additional energy. Try not to make a special fuss over sweet foods so that your children do not come to think of them as rewards or as special activities when they feel bored. Research has shown that when we use sweet foods as a reward, we reinforce children's desires for them.

Supplements

Many parents use multivitamin supplements as a form of insurance to make themselves feel secure that their children have received their share of vitamins each day. But evidence would suggest that this is unnecessary when children eat the recommended intake of foods from all four food groups. Moreover, there are risks associated with overdoses of multivitamin supplements. Because they come in brightly coloured packages and have sweet flavours, children think that they are candies. Every year there are cases of children who were tempted to eat many tablets at once. If you find half a bottle missing, take your child immediately to a hospital to prevent the consequences of overdose.

When do children need supplements? You should recognize the food patterns that lead to malnutrition so that you will know whether your children are getting insufficient nutrients from their food. In North America the most common nutrient deficiencies are iron and calcium. Iron deficiency is most common for children who are consuming a diet that contains little or no meat or iron-fortified bread, grain, or cereals. The iron in meat products is best because it is very easily absorbed. Fish and seafood, particularly oysters, clams, and mussels, are good sources of iron. However, children are often reluctant to eat meats and it is useful to encourage them to eat breads and cereals that are fortified with iron. Green leafy vegetables such as dark lettuce, spinach, and broccoli also contain a good amount of iron. If you notice symptoms such as constant tiredness, pale membranes around the eyes, or pale tissue under the nail bed, it is time for your child to be evaluated for iron deficiency anemia. One indicator of iron deficiency is that the child may try to eat nonfoods such as ice or food from the family pet's dish. These activities are referred to as "pica" and may be indicators of iron deficiency anemia. The desire for ice is a good example of the lack of body wisdom for nutrients. There is no iron in ice and no physiological explanation for this craving. If anemia is diagnosed by the physician, then the child will be placed on iron supplements to ensure adequate iron nutrition.

Research in countries where iron deficiency is high has demonstrated that children's cognitive ability and performance improve when iron is added to their diet. It is estimated that as many as 10 percent of children in the United States and in Canada are iron deficient. It is worth pursuing this issue with your pediatrician or family physician if you have any reason to suspect that your child is iron deficient. But first, look at the typical daily intake of your child to see whether she is getting enough meat or meat alternatives such as lima beans, soy beans, or kidney beans. Other good sources include dried fruits such as peaches, apricots, and prunes. One of our favourite iron-rich foods is a soup made with split peas and beans with added vegetables such as carrots (see page 225). This combination gives children a very good source of iron and makes a nice alternative to sandwiches at lunch time.

To improve the absorption of iron in your child's diet, encourage him to eat foods that contain vitamin C. Vitamin C enhances iron absorption as do natural factors in meat, fish, and poultry. Another excellent way of getting iron into the diet is to cook with an iron skillet. The iron in the cookware actually adds iron to the foods that are prepared in it. Foods that are acidic such as spaghetti sauce or a chili dinner are enhanced dramatically by the use of iron cookware. Although cast iron pots are rather heavy to cook with, they can make a significant contribution to the overall intake of iron by the family.

Calcium is another nutrient of concern, particularly for children and adolescents. During periods of rapid growth, it is important for children to lay down a good bone mass. One of the best sources of calcium is milk, not just because the milk provides calcium but also because milk is fortified with vitamin D, which is essential for the absorption of calcium. If children do not like milk there is no harm in adding chocolate powder to get them to drink it. Although chocolate can reduce the absorption of calcium, the small amount added to a cup of milk, which is already rich in calcium, will not significantly reduce the calcium available to children. The child is far better off drinking milk with some chocolate added than not drinking milk at all.

Good sources of calcium include the bones of fish such as canned sardines or canned salmon. Other good sources include green vegetables such as broccoli and seeds such as sesame seeds. However, the best source of calcium is milk and dairy products, including cheese, yogurt, and even ice cream. Keep in mind cottage cheese and cream cheese are not very good sources of calcium. Cottage cheese is a reasonable source only when milk liquids are added back to the curds of the cottage cheese.

Children who are lactose intolerant should drink milk that has had the lactose removed from it or take enzymes that help to break down lactose. Young children are not commonly lactose intolerant. The condition usually develops in adolescence. Nevertheless, if your child has gas, bloating, or diarrhea after drinking milk, then it is worth investigating to find out if lactose intolerance is the problem. If this diagnosis is confirmed, get advice from a dietitian. Your child may be able to tolerate small amounts of milk without experiencing any discomfort. She can also get calcium from milk products that have been fermented. Foods such as yogurt as well as hard cheeses such as Swiss, Cheddar, and Muenster are all produced by the action of bacteria that use up the lactose in their own metabolism. It is important to read the labels of yogurt in particular, because some products are simply milk-based blends with some yogurt flavour added to them.

If your child has a real allergy to milk, getting enough calcium may be more difficult, because it is the protein portion of milk to which she reacts and she will not be able to tolerate any milk products. Again, get advice from an experienced dietitian. You can give your child green leafy vegetables such as turnip greens, broccoli, and bok choy, and offer tofu to enhance her calcium intake. Children who have a milk allergy should also be evaluated to determine whether a calcium supplement is necessary. Consideration should be given to a vitamin D supplement to go along with it. This decision will be based on how much sunshine children are exposed to. Given our need to protect children from the sun, a vitamin D supplement may be necessary.

Vegetarian Diets for Children

Children raised on vegetarian diets tend to be smaller than their peers who are not. They have no more or fewer colds or childhood illnesses than their peers, but their diet does require some special attention. There are different types of vegetarians. Those who eat fish, milk, and eggs are likely to get a good variety of nutrients. Although iron is best absorbed from meats, with adequate fish, beans, and fortified breads and cereals, these children may not need a supplement. Children who eat no fish or animal-based products whatsoever may not get enough iron, calcium, and vitamin B_{12}. Meal planning for these children should pay special attention to combining grains, legumes, nuts, and seeds to get a good protein intake. A session with a dietitian would be especially worthwhile for parents of strictly vegetarian children. Monitoring their diet and their growth and development would also be a good idea.

Coping with Food Messages in the Media

Television has many different roles to play in shaping children's attitudes towards food and health. Television commercials create demands for foods that are low in nutrients but are promoted as fun to eat, magical to purchase, or valuable to your social life. The messages from television also tell us that successful people are slim yet manage to spend a good part of their day eating and drinking.

Recent studies have shown that there is a significant difference between young couch potatoes and their more active peers in terms of the average degree of obesity. When children are watching television they are physically inactive. At the same time, they are exposed to products that are high in calories and low in nutrients and are likely to eat recreationally. They do not eat because they are hungry but because they need something to do.

Children do not understand that the purpose of television programs is to bring the audience to the advertiser in order to promote a specific product. They need to be educated to be better consumers. As a result of television watching, children often put pressure on their parents to buy the products that they have seen advertised. Shopping for groceries with young children can only lead to embarrassing battles in the supermarket or to regrettable decisions at the cash register. As children get older (around five or six years of age), grocery shopping may provide them with an opportunity to learn about making choices. If they have several requests for breakfast cereals or snacks, let them choose one or two options for that week. As children begin to read and do mathematics, use the shopping trip to reinforce their skills. Ultimately, however, parents need to work with their children to decide which foods will be purchased and served at home. This forms the basic diet for the family. A well-balanced diet based on a variety of healthy foods will help to establish a sound nutritious diet for every member of the family.

RECIPES

T HE RECIPES IN THIS SECTION WERE SELECTED WITH THE WHOLE family in mind. Younger and older members of the family need to have foods that are interesting, nutritious, and easy to prepare. The menu planner's worst nightmare is realizing that there are only three recipes that all members of the family enjoy; this leads either to supreme boredom or to the "restaurant syndrome" (everyone has a different meal at the same table). Our goal is to expand your family's repertoire.

In general, children prefer foods that are identifiable (no mysteries allowed), crunchy or crispy in texture, and sweet or bland in taste. These recipes attempt to meet all those demands but we know that it isn't easy. To balance some of the more adventurous recipes, we suggest some simple but familiar accompaniments. It is generally more comforting for children to try one new recipe at a time, especially when it is in the company of some favourite foods.

One great way to get children to try new foods is to involve them in the preparation of the recipes. Watching the ingredients go into a new recipe helps to remove some of the mystery. Try to get the whole family involved in planning the weekly menu. Sit down together once a week and decide as a group what to have for dinner each night. Getting everyone to buy into the plan leaves no surprises for the eaters and no disappointments for the cook. Post your weekly menu on the fridge to help you organize your shopping and to stick with your plan.

Depending on their age, activity, and appetite, children are encouraged to select from the minimum number of servings suggested by *Canada's Food Guide to Healthy Eating*. For example, a four-year-old might select five servings of grains throughout the day whereas a twelve-year-old might double that intake. The key is to balance the food groups and select a variety of foods. A typical menu for these two age groups is provided to show how some of these recipes can help you apply the food guide for each child's needs. The actual serving sizes are very important and are described in each section that follows.

	Four-year-old boy	Twelve-year-old girl
Grain products	5 servings	10 servings
Vegetables and fruits	5 servings	8 servings
Milk products	2 servings	3 servings
Meat and alternates	2 servings	3 servings

The guidelines were designed for children four years and older. For younger children, the guidelines can be adapted by reducing the serving sizes by about half. The need for variety is the same but it is most important to match the food intake to the child's appetite. Meals and snacks both contribute to a child's overall nutrient intake. For this reason, we have included some great snack foods to help balance the total day's food plan.

Grain Products

The guidelines recommend 5–12 servings of grain products each day. A serving size is defined as one slice of bread, $\frac{2}{3}$ cup (150 mL) of cereal, or $\frac{1}{2}$ cup (125 mL) of pasta or rice. Keep in mind that the total number required daily will depend on each child's needs and appetite. During rapid growth spurts or on very active days, children may have an appetite for more. When growth and activity slow down, so does the appetite. Encourage your child to stay in touch with his energy needs by being aware of his own appetite. Provide a variety of nutritious foods and let him respond to his hunger. Don't force him to eat or make an issue out of it. Let nature take its course.

Most children don't need much encouragement to eat the foods in the grain group. These foods include rice, pasta, breads, ready-to-eat and cooked cereals, muffins, pancakes, and other products made from grains or flours. They provide an important source of starch, fibre, vitamins (thiamin, niacin, and riboflavin), and minerals (iron, zinc, and magnesium) and should be whole grains whenever possible to get maximum nutritional value.

Incorporate cereals into snack foods such as Oatmeal Cookies (page 256), Nuts and Bolts Mix (page 256), and Peanut Butter Krispies (page 264) to add grains between meals.

Vegetables and Fruit

Parents often fret over their children's lack of interest in vegetables. When I ask them if they were vegetable lovers as children, the answer is usually no. Further probing often reveals that the child does like certain vegetables and is very fond of fruit. Most kids like fruit and it pays to remember that this food group does include both. There is no reason to force your child to eat vegetables when a glass of orange juice, some carrot sticks, and three other fruits will provide the same nutrients. Add new fruits to the repertoire whenever you can, but always try a sample before introducing a new fruit to your child to make sure that it is at the peak of flavour. An unripe or overripe fruit will increase the chance that they'll never eat that fruit again.

The recommendation for this food group is 5–10 servings of

fruits and vegetables a day. A serving is one medium-sized fruit or vegetable, 1 cup (250 mL) of salad, or ½ cup (125 mL) of cooked vegetable. Five servings would be reasonable for a younger child and 10 servings for teenagers. These servings can be met with recipes found throughout this section, including soups, frozen fruit juice, and vegetables with dip. We have also hidden vegetables in some of the more adventurous combination foods such as Easy Pita Pizzas (page 244), Vietnamese Salad Rolls (page 229), and Lazy Gourmet Salsa (page 219). Think about the foods that your child enjoys most and make them available. Try some of these exciting new recipes when the time seems right and you'll be pleased with the results.

Milk Products

Milk is the sole food for all newborns and continues to be an important source of protein, calcium, and vitamin D for children and adults. Two to three servings are recommended for children aged four to nine years and three to four servings for those aged ten to sixteen. A serving is defined as 1 cup (250 mL) of milk, ¾ cup (175 mL) of yogurt, or a 2 oz (60 g) serving of cheese. Discuss problems of lactose intolerance or milk allergy with a dietitian.

This section provides many exciting ways to serve milk products as snacks, soups, or desserts. Try them all.

Meat and Alternatives

The meat and alternatives group includes poultry, meat, fish, legumes, and eggs. This food group is an important source of protein, fat (we all need some!), iron, and B vitamins.

When many of today's parents were growing up, their own parents tended to follow the pattern of "pushing" meats. They were considered valuable sources of protein, and, because of the high cost they added to the grocery bill, no parent could stand to see them go to waste. Fortunately, there are very few documented cases of protein deficiency in Canadian children. In fact, most of them get twice the daily minimum requirement of protein with two to three servings per day from the meat and alternatives food group and the recommended intake from the milk group. Keep in mind the serving size of 2–4 oz (60–125 g).

While most children object to one or more of these foods at some point, the group offers a wide range of choices. If your child dislikes the strong flavour of certain meats, try using ground meats in chili or tostados. Most butchers will grind veal, chicken, or pork for an alternative to beef in these recipes.

Try the legume and tofu recipes and remember that peanut butter, on its own or in a sauce, counts towards the meat and alternatives food group.

Sauces

We have included various sauces in this section because they add flavour and nutrition to the simplest recipes. Children can acquire a taste for any one of these as easily as they do for ketchup! Whether the sauce is based on peanut butter, beans, or seeds, it is a good source of protein and fibre. All sauces should be kept in the refrigerator.

Try this menu plan to provide the full set of recommended food groups. It is a plan the whole family will enjoy!

Breakfast
juice or fruit
Breakfast Porridge *(p. 212)*
Easy Banana-Walnut Muffin *(p. 215)*
$^1/_2$ cup (125 mL) milk

Lunch
Family Fish Chowder *(p. 221)*
fresh roll
Peanut Butter Krispie *(p. 264)*
sliced green apple

Snack
Oatmeal Cookie *(p. 256)*
Peach Smoothie *(p. 269)*

Dinner

Vietnamese Salad Roll *(p. 229)*

Lyla's Cranberry Chicken *(p. 249)*

Vegetable Fried Rice with Tofu *(p. 110)*

Snack

Frozen Fruit Pop *(p. 266)*

Tahini Garlic Dip or Dressing

Tahini is a great nondairy sauce or dip for vegetables or crackers. Feel free to adjust the garlic to taste.

$\frac{1}{2}$–$\frac{3}{4}$ cup (175 mL) water

$\frac{1}{2}$ cup (125 mL) tahini

$\frac{1}{4}$ cup (50 mL) lemon juice

2 tsp (10 mL) low-sodium soy sauce

2 cloves garlic, minced

Salt and pepper to taste

Place all ingredients in blender, and blend until creamy.

Makes 1$\frac{1}{2}$ cups (325 mL).

Teriyaki Sauce

This sauce is our family's favourite for salmon. I marinate 1$\frac{1}{2}$ lbs (750 g) of salmon for 5–10 minutes and then broil or grill the salmon on the barbecue.

$\frac{3}{4}$ cup (175 mL) low-sodium soy sauce

2 tbsp (25 mL) rice vinegar or sherry

1 tbsp (10 mL) brown sugar

1 tbsp (15 mL) minced gingerroot

1 tsp (5 mL) sesame oil

3 cloves garlic, minced

Mix all ingredients together.

Makes approximately 1 cup (250 mL).

Hoisin Sauce

This is traditionally served as a dipping sauce for cooked meats and salad rolls.

4 tbsp (25 mL) low-sodium soy sauce	Mix all ingredients together.
4 tbsp (25 mL) hoisin sauce	
2 tbsp (15 mL) rice vinegar	
1 tbsp (10 mL) brown sugar	
2 tsp (5 mL) grated gingerroot	
4 cloves garlic, minced	
	Makes ⅔ cup (150 mL).

Michiko's Miso Sauce

This is the sauce that everyone expects on vegetables when they come to our house for dinner. Miso can be found in Japanese specialty stores and health food stores. It's full of protein and delicious. The sauce will keep in the refrigerator for up to one month.

7 oz (200 g) mild miso	Combine all ingredients in a food processor and process until smooth.
⅔ cup (150 mL) mirin	
½ cup (125 mL) sesame seeds, roasted and ground	
¼ cup (50 mL) granulated sugar	
¼ cup (50 mL) rice vinegar	
2½ tbsp (35 mL) sesame oil	
1 tbsp (15 mL) hot Szechuan paste	
8 to 10 cloves garlic	
	Serve over hot or cold asparagus, green beans, or mixed vegetables. Also great as a dipping sauce.
	Makes 4 cups (1L).

Hummus

This Middle Eastern treat is high in protein and fibre. Kids love it at snack time. Great as a dip for pita and hearty breads as well as vegetables.

2 cans (each 14 oz/398 mL) chickpeas, drained and rinsed ¾ cup (175 mL) water 3 tbsp (50 mL) lemon juice 2–3 cloves garlic, minced ½ tsp (2 mL) salt	Process all ingredients in food processor for 2 minutes.
½ cup (125 mL) tahini	Gradually add to above and process until thick. (Add more tahini or more water depending on your desired consistency.)
	MAKES 5–6 CUPS (1.5L). SERVES 8–10.

Tzatziki

Tzatziki is a light Mediterranean sauce that's great with everything from raw vegetables to vegetarian burgers.

2 cups (500 mL) plain yogurt ½ cup (125 mL) finely chopped English cucumber 1 tbsp (15 mL) chopped fresh dill or mint 1 tsp (5 mL) minced garlic Salt and pepper to taste	Mix together.
	MAKES 2 CUPS (500 ML).

Spicy Peanut Sauce

This is a versatile sauce for dipping, barbecuing, or pouring over rice-and-vegetable combinations.

4 tbsp (50 mL) peanut butter

4 tbsp (50 mL) water

3 tbsp (50 mL) rice vinegar

3 tbsp (50 mL) vegetable oil

2 tbsp (25 mL) low-sodium soy sauce

2 tbsp (25 mL) lime juice

2 tbsp (25 mL) hoisin sauce

1 tbsp (15 mL) sesame oil

1 tsp (5 mL) Chinese chili garlic sauce

In saucepan, bring all ingredients to a boil, reduce heat, and simmer 1 minute.

MAKES 1 CUP (250 ML).

Rena's Berry Bran Muffins

The goodness of bran, wheat germ, and flax seeds enhanced by the bright flavours of blueberries and cranberries. What a way to start your children's day! Good for packing into lunches too.

1 cup (250 mL) brown sugar 1 cup (250 mL) buttermilk ½ cup (125 mL) canola oil or vegetable oil 1 egg 2 tbsp (25 mL) molasses	Combine in a large bowl.
1½ cups (375 mL) natural bran ⅔ cup (250 mL) all-purpose flour ⅓ cup (250 mL) wheat germ ¼ cup (50 mL) flax seeds, ground ¼ cup (50 mL) sesame seeds, toasted 1 tsp (5 mL) baking soda ½ tsp (2 mL) salt ½ tsp (2 mL) cinnamon	Mix together, then add to brown sugar–buttermilk mixture.
½ cup (125 mL) blueberries, fresh or frozen ½ cup (125 mL) cranberries, fresh or frozen	Gently fold into batter.
	Spoon batter into paper-cup lined muffin tin. Bake in 400°F (200°C) oven 18–20 minutes until top springs back when lightly touched
	MAKES 1 DOZEN MUFFINS.

Pumpkin Bread

Pumpkin is a good source of beta carotene. This bread is a great after-school snack and can be made year-round.

2 cups (500 mL) all-purpose flour 2 tsp (10 mL) baking powder ¼ tsp (1 mL) salt ¼ tsp (1 mL) cinnamon ¼ tsp (1 mL) ground ginger ¼ tsp (1 mL) baking soda Pinch ground cloves Pinch grated nutmeg	Mix together and set aside.
1 cup (250 mL) brown sugar ⅓ cup (75 mL) shortening	Cream shortening and sugar.
2 eggs	Add one at a time to sugar, beating each time.
1 cup (250 mL) canned pumpkin ¼ cup (50 mL) 2% milk	Mix into sugar-egg mixture.
	Add dry ingredients to pumpkin mixture and stir until just smooth. Pour into greased loaf pan. Bake in 350°F (180°C) oven for 1 hour, or until tester inserted in centre comes out clean. SERVES 8.

Oatmeal Pancakes

Pancakes are always a favourite and these have a great texture as well.

1 cup (250 mL) quick-cooking rolled oats 2 cups (500 mL) 2% milk	Soak oats in milk for 10 minutes.
1 egg, beaten ¼ cup (50 mL) vegetable oil	Add to oats and whisk to combine.
1 cup (250 mL) all-purpose flour 2 tbsp (25 mL) brown sugar 1 tbsp (15 mL) baking powder ½ tsp (2 mL) salt ½ tsp (2 mL) cinnamon	Mix together dry ingredients. Add to oat mixture and mix to combine.
	Heat nonstick skillet over medium heat. Add a little margarine to lightly grease. Drop batter by spoonfuls onto skillet. When bubbles begin to form on surface, flip and cook until lightly browned. Serve with Cinnamon-Honey Butter (see below). SERVES 6.

Cinnamon-Honey Butter

Mira loves to make this for breakfast with toast and pancakes.

½ cup (125 mL) soft butter or margarine ½ cup (125 mL) liquid honey 2–3 tbsp (50 mL) cinnamon	Mix well. Spread onto pancakes.
	MAKES 1 CUP.

Breakfast Porridge

Oatmeal is a great source of soluble fibre and starch. Kids love oatmeal so get them started when they're young. Brown sugar helps bring out the best in it.

2 cups (500 mL) water ¼ tsp (1 mL) salt	Bring water to a boil in saucepan.
1 cup (250 mL) quick-cooking rolled oats	Add to water. Stir and cook for 1 minute. Reduce heat—cover and cook on low for 15 minutes, or until water is absorbed.
	Sprinkle with brown sugar and serve with cream or milk and fresh fruit. SERVES 3–4.

To make individual bowls in microwave:

⅔ cup (150 mL) water ⅓ cup (75 mL) quick-cooking rolled oats	Mix together in bowl. Cover bowl with plastic wrap. Cook on High for 1 minute. Stir. Return and cook on High for 30 seconds. Let stand 1 minute in microwave.

Granola for Kids

Get your kids to help you make this easy recipe. They will want to eat it for breakfast every day. Serve it with milk or yogurt and fresh fruit for a complete meal, or use it as a topping for ice milk.

5 cups (1.25 L) quick-cooking rolled oats 1 cup (250 mL) wheat germ 1 cup (250 mL) wheat or rye flakes 1 cup (250 mL) sunflower seeds, hulled 1 cup (250 mL) unsweetened coconut 1 cup (250 mL) almonds, cashews, or walnut pieces ½ cup (125 mL) sesame seeds	Mix together.
1 cup (250 mL) liquid honey ½ cup (125 mL) light oil	Combine and add to oat mixture. Stir thoroughly.
	Spread the mixture evenly on a large cookie sheet. Bake at 325°F (160°C) for 10 minutes. Remove from oven and turn mixture to toast other side. Return to oven and repeat process twice. (Entire baking time is approximately 45 minutes.) Mixture should be toasted completely. Cool and add 2 cups (500 mL) raisins. Makes 3 qts (3 L).

Oatmeal-Blueberry Scones

Serve these warm as an after-school snack with a glass of cold milk.

2 cups (500 mL) all-purpose flour ½ cup (125 mL) quick-cooking rolled oats ¼ cup (50 mL) granulated sugar 1 tbsp (15 mL) baking powder ½ tsp (2 mL) salt	Mix dry ingredients in bowl.
½ cup (125 mL) butter	Cut into small pieces and add to flour. Mix with fingertips until a coarse meal is formed.
2 eggs, beaten ½ cup (125 mL) light cream	Mix together and add to flour-oatmeal mixture to form dough. Knead for 1 minute.
½ cup (125 mL) fresh or frozen blueberries	Add and mix into dough with a wooden spoon.
	Divide dough into 2 parts. Roll each into a circle ½-inch (1 cm) thick. Cut into 8 wedge-shaped pieces. Place on buttered cookie sheet. Bake at 425°F (220°C) for 14–15 minutes, or until golden. MAKES 16 SCONES.

Easy Banana-Walnut Muffins

This is as easy as it gets! Great for breakfast or send to school for lunch or a snack.

2 cups (500 mL) all-purpose flour 1 ½ tsp (7 mL) baking soda	Sift together.
3 eggs, beaten 3 ripe bananas, mashed 1 ¼ cups (375 mL) granulated sugar ½ cup (125 mL) vegetable oil ½ cup (125 mL) chopped walnuts	Combine thoroughly, then add to flour mixture and stir until just blended.
	Butter muffin tin, or use paper liners. Fill each muffin tin ⅔ full. Bake at 400°F (200°C) for 20 minutes, or until tops of muffins spring back when lightly touched. MAKES ONE DOZEN.

Cornbread

Kids love this served warm with butter or margarine.

1 cup (250 mL) cornmeal ½ cup (125 mL) all-purpose flour 2 tbsp (25 mL) granulated sugar 1 tbsp (15 mL) baking powder 1 tsp (5 mL) salt	Combine dry ingredients in bowl and mix well.
1 egg, beaten 1½ cups (375 mL) 2% milk	Mix together and add to dry ingredients.
2 tbsp (25 mL) melted butter	Add to cornmeal mixture and mix until blended.
	Pour into buttered 9-inch (2.5 L) square pan. Bake at 375°F (190°C) for 25–30 minutes, or until tester inserted in centre comes out clean. SERVES 6.

Raw Vegetables and Dill Dip

Other suggestions for dips include Spicy Peanut Sauce (page 208), Tahini Garlic Dip (page 205), Hummus (page 207), and Tzatziki (page 207).

Carrot sticks Snow peas Broccoli florets Celery stalks Cucumber slices Snap peas Red pepper strips	Wash vegetables well and arrange on a platter.
½ cup (125 mL) mayonnaise ½ cup (125 mL) plain yogurt ½–1 tsp (2–5 mL) dried dill or 1 tbsp (15 mL) chopped fresh dill ¼ tsp (1 mL) salt Pepper to taste	Mix ingredients together in bowl.
1–2 tbsp (15–25 mL) ketchup (optional)	Add for a pink sauce.
	Makes 1 cup (250 mL) sauce.

Nachos

Here is a fun way to serve vegetables without alarming the kids.
Try Lazy Gourmet Salsa (page 219).

1 bag (10 oz/284 mL) tortilla chips 6 oz (150 g) Cheddar cheese, grated	Place 2–3 handfuls of tortilla chips onto plate and sprinkle with cheese. Microwave at Medium High for 1 minute, or until cheese has melted.
1 cup (250 mL) salsa ½ cup (125 mL) chopped tomatoes ½ cup (125 mL) chopped olives ½ cup (125 mL) chopped cucumbers ½ cup (125 mL) seeded and chopped green pepper	Put each topping into separate bowls and serve with nachos.
	Serve with 1 cup (250 mL) each guacamole and sour cream. SERVES 6.

Lazy Gourmet Salsa

Tomatoes are not always a favourite with children, but for some reason, most kids enjoy salsa. This is a much-coveted recipe from The Lazy Gourmet. The original was given to me by Jane Mundy who caters to the movies in Vancouver. It's always a big hit. Feel free to make it more or less spicy with the jalapeño peppers. It's a good source of vitamin C.

1 can (14 oz/398 mL) whole tomatoes

1 can (14 oz/398 mL) crushed tomatoes

2 tbsp (25 mL) lemon juice

1–2 tbsp (15–25 mL) chopped cilantro

2 tsp (10 mL) jalapeño juice

2 jalapeño peppers, chopped

1 small onion, chopped

½ green pepper, seeded and chopped

3–4 cloves garlic, minced

Combine all ingredients in food processor and process until you reach the desired consistency.

MAKES 4 CUPS (1L) SAUCE.

Hearty Vegetable Chowder

Vegetable soup is a wonderful way to boost vegetable eating. Somehow, the kids don't notice how many they've consumed.

1 small onion, chopped fine 2 tbsp (25 mL) butter	Sauté onion in butter until tender.
2 carrots, peeled and chopped 1 stalk celery, chopped	Add to onion and cook 5 more minutes.
1 medium potato, peeled and chopped	Add to onion and vegetables.
2 cups (500 mL) water 1 cup (250 mL) frozen corn kernels 1 tsp (5 mL) salt $\frac{1}{4}$ tsp (1 mL) pepper	Add, cover, and simmer over low heat for 25 minutes.
2 cups (500 mL) 2% milk	Add just before serving and heat thoroughly. Pour into bowls.
1 cup (250 mL) grated Cheddar cheese	Sprinkle each bowl with grated cheese.
	SERVES 4.

Family Fish Chowder

This is a great combination of many of our favourite foods put together into one comfort food for a cold winter's night. Feel free to modify and add your own favourite vegetables and fish.

1 cup (250 mL) chopped onions 3 tbsp (50 mL) butter	Sauté onions in butter until tender.
3 tbsp (50 mL) all-purpose flour	Add to onions and stir for at least 1 minute.
3 cups (750 mL) 2% milk	Slowly add milk, stirring constantly.
1½ lbs (750 g) halibut, cut in pieces 1 cup (250 mL) vegetable stock 1 cup (250 mL) frozen corn kernels 1 cup (250 mL) frozen peas 8 small new potatoes, chopped 2 carrots, peeled and chopped 2 stalks celery, chopped 1 red pepper, seeded and chopped 1 tbsp (15 mL) chopped fresh parsley ½ tsp (2 mL) dried marjoram ½ tsp (2 mL) dried basil ½ tsp (2 mL) dried dill Salt and pepper to taste	Add and simmer for 15 minutes.
	SERVES 6.

Mama Rozzie's Chicken Soup with Matzoh Balls

This is the classic Jewish comfort food. It continues to work wonders. Chicken fat used to be credited as the source of "tam" or flavour in Jewish food. Nowadays we let the soup get to room temperature, then skim off the fat and discard it.

2 chicken fryers, each 3 lb (1.5 kg)	Put chickens in large pot and cover with water. Bring to a boil, skim off fat, reduce heat to low, and simmer for 30 minutes. Skim off fat again. Add more water to cover chickens, filling pot ⅔ full with water.
8 carrots, washed and halved 3 large white onions, whole 1 bunch celery, cut into 6-inch (15 cm) pieces 1 red pepper, halved 1 tbsp (15 mL) chopped fresh parsley 1 tbsp (15 mL) chopped fresh dill	Add to above and simmer over low heat for about 2 hours, or until chicken is tender.
	Remove chicken and vegetables from pot, and strain liquid through colander lined with a cheese cloth into another pot. Skin and bone chicken, and add meat back to soup. Serve with egg noodles or matzoh balls. SERVES 8, OR 2 PEOPLE WITH COLDS!

Mama Rozzie's Matzoh Balls

We've all been proud of our mother Rozzie's matzoh balls and none of us has yet matched the light texture of them. If the egg whites fall, you might as well plan a baseball game to use up the uneaten balls.

3 egg whites Pinch salt	Beat egg whites with salt until peaks form.
3 egg yolks	Beat well and fold into egg whites.
½ cup (125 mL) matzoh meal	Stir into eggs and let sit in fridge for 2 hours, or until mixture has gone flat.
	Fill a saucepan ⅔ with cold water. Bring water to a boil. Wet hands and form the matzoh mixture into small balls the size of walnuts. Drop balls into boiling water, reduce heat to low and simmer for 30–40 minutes. Remove with slotted spoon and add to chicken soup. MAKES 8 MATZOH BALLS.

Miso Soup with Tofu

Mira loves to pick out and devour the tofu in this highly nutritious soup; she says it's her favourite soup. Miso can be found in Asian specialty stores. It should be refrigerated at all times. Experiment at home to get the flavour that most suits your family. There are lots of different misos on the market. The darker the colour, the stronger the flavour.

8 cups (2 L) water 1 cup (250 mL) thinly sliced onions 2 medium carrots, peeled and cut in thin strips 3 tbsp (50 mL) low-sodium soy sauce 1½ tsp (7 mL) grated gingerroot	Bring water to boil, add vegetables, soy, and ginger, then reduce heat and simmer for 30 minutes.
3 tbsp (50 mL) miso	Remove ¼–⅓ cup (50–75 mL) of vegetable broth and add to miso to make a paste. Return paste to broth. Simmer without boiling for a few minutes longer.
½ lb (250 g) tofu, chopped in small pieces	Add and simmer 1 minute longer.
½ cup (125 mL) chopped green onion	Serve and sprinkle soup with green onion.
	SERVES 6–8.

Split Pea and Barley Soup

This makes a great meal for a school lunch. Put it in a food jar, add a fresh bagel, and a crisp apple, and your kids will sail through the afternoon.

10 cups (2.5 L) water

¾ cup (175 mL) split green peas

¼ cup (50 mL) yellow peas

¼ cup (50 mL) lima beans

¼ cup (50 mL) pearl barley

¼ cup (50 mL) seeded and chopped red pepper

2 carrots, peeled and chopped

2 stalks celery, chopped

2 cloves garlic, minced

1 onion, chopped

1 large marrow bone or 1 tbsp (15 mL) powdered chicken stock

1 tsp (5 mL) salt

½ tsp (2 mL) pepper

½ tsp (2 mL) turmeric

¼ tsp (1 mL) paprika

Put all ingredients into large pot. Cover and bring to a boil over high heat. Reduce heat to low and simmer for 3 hours.

SERVES 8.

Chappati Roll-Ups

This is a variation of one of the hottest items on the market for healthful eating in Vancouver. Play with varieties of vegetables and sauces. Pesto sauce adds an Italian flavour and salsa adds a Mexican flavour.

6 chappatis or rotis 4 cups (1 L) cooked brown rice, warm	Place ⅔ cup (150 mL) brown rice along bottom of each chappati, leaving 2 inches (5 cm) of chappati on each side to be folded over.
2 cups (500 mL) grated carrots 10 oz (300 g) chopped cooked chicken 1 cup (250 mL) seeded and grated red pepper 1 cup (250 mL) mung bean sprouts 1 cup (250 mL) chopped spinach leaves	Top rice with ⅙ of each of the vegetables.
¾–1 cup (175–250 mL) Spicy Peanut Sauce (p. 208)	Pour 2–3 tbsp (25–50 mL) of peanut sauce on top. Fold over sides of chappati and roll up.
	MAKES 6.

Tomato and Cheese Strata

Notice how there is nothing in here that the kids are likely to complain about. Feel free to use a canned tomato sauce instead of the fresh tomato sauce.

1 tbsp (15 mL) butter 1 tbsp (25 mL) olive oil 1 medium onion, chopped	Sauté onion in butter and oil until translucent.
4 cups (1 L) peeled, seeded, and chopped tomatoes 3 cloves garlic, minced Bay leaf	Add to onion and cook for about 20 minutes, or until sauce is a chunky purée. Discard bay leaf. Run sauce through food processor or blender.
1 loaf day-old French bread 3 cups (750 mL) 2% milk	Grease 13- x 9-inch (3.5 L) casserole. Cut bread into 27 pieces. Dip bread into milk to soften. Arrange 9 slices of bread on bottom of casserole. Spread 1 cup (250 mL) tomato sauce on top.
½ lb (250 g) mozzarella cheese, thinly sliced ½ lb (250 g) fontina cheese, thinly sliced	Arrange half the cheese over sauce. Repeat with another layer of bread, sauce, and cheese. Top with last 9 slices of bread and remaining sauce.
6 eggs, well beaten 3–4 tbsp (50–60 mL) grated Parmesan cheese 1 tbsp (15 mL) butter	Pour eggs over casserole, piercing bread with tip of knife until eggs are absorbed. Sprinkle with Parmesan and dot with butter. Let stand ½ hour, or until eggs are absorbed.
	Bake at 375°F (190°C) for about 45 minutes, or until set. SERVES 8–10.

Cheese Quesadillas

Rena makes her quesadillas with 1 tbsp (15 mL) of pesto and 2 oz (50 g) low-fat Monterey Jack cheese between two tortillas. She then puts the quesadilla into an ungreased skillet, and heats it over medium heat for three minutes on each side until the cheese is melted and the tortilla is crispy. A delicious lunch with a tossed salad. Experiment and try your favourite fillings. Use leftovers, or ask your kids what they would like in their quesadillas. It's a great change from the traditional grilled cheese sandwich!

10 5-inch (12 cm) flour tortillas 1 egg, beaten	Place five tortillas on counter. Brush each on top with egg.
2 cups (500 mL) grated Swiss cheese 1 cup (250 mL) light cream cheese ½ red onion, chopped ½ red pepper, seeded and chopped fine 1 jalapeño pepper, seeded and chopped fine (optional)	Mix all ingredients for filling together.
	Spread ⅕ of filling on top of each tortilla. Place another tortilla on top of cheese mixture. Press gently. Brush remaining egg on top and press around edges to seal. Bake in 350°F (180°C) oven for about 10 minutes, or until golden. Remove from oven. Let sit 3 minutes, then cut into triangles. Serve with Lazy Gourmet Salsa (p. 219).
	MAKES 5 QUESADILLAS

Vietnamese Salad Rolls

This recipe was originally given to me by South China Seas Food Shop in Granville Island Market. Most rice paper wrappers are imported from Thailand. You can find them in many Asian food stores. When removed from the package, the papers curl up, so keep them wrapped before you use them.

Ingredients	Instructions
6–8 oz (175–225 g) rice vermicelli	Bring pot of water to a boil. Add vermicelli, turn off heat, and let noodles soak for 5 minutes. Rinse with water and drain. Set aside.
8 rice paper wrappers	Fill a large bowl with warm water. Immerse one rice paper wrapper in the water for 5 seconds, or until softened. Remove to plate. Fold over the bottom ⅓ of the wrapper.
8–12 lettuce leaves	Put one or two lettuce leaves on the folded wrapper and put about 1 oz (25 g) vermicelli on top. Fold up slightly.
1 cup (250 mL) grated carrot 8 oz (200 g) cooked shrimp or cooked chicken	Put about 2 tbsp (25 mL) of carrots and 1 oz (25 g) shrimp or chicken on the lettuce.
8 green onions, trimmed	Add the green onion in front of the vermicelli so that it will protrude from the finished roll. Roll the folded bottom edge away from you, enveloping the ingredients and making a tight roll. Repeat with the remaining wrappers. Keep in a cool, moist place until serving time. Serve with satay sauce or Hoisin Sauce (p. 206).

MAKES 8 ROLLS.

Chicken, Shrimp, and Beef Satays with Peanut Sauce

This food is fun to eat and kids should also have a variety of sauces for dipping. It makes everyone feel as if they're in a restaurant and it's not much effort. To make these satays, you'll need 36 bamboo skewers. Soak the skewers in water while the meat is marinating. (This prevents slivers and burning on the barbeque.)

Marinade: 1 cup (250 mL) low-sodium soy sauce 3 tbsp (50 mL) grated gingerroot 3 tbsp (50 mL) sherry 3 tbsp (50 mL) freshly squeezed lime juice 2 tbsp (25 mL) brown sugar 4 cloves garlic, minced	Combine in glass dish. Divide into 3 small bowls.
24 uncooked shrimp, peeled and deveined 1 lb (500 g) boneless chicken breasts, cut in ½-inch (1 cm) strips 1 lb (500 g) beef steak, cut in 3- x ½-inch (7.5 x 1 cm) strips	Marinate shrimp, beef, and chicken separately in the 3 bowls; cover and chill for 30 minutes.
	Thread shrimp, chicken, and beef on separate skewers. Grill about 3 minutes on each side. Chicken takes a little longer, shrimp will be done when curled and pink. Serve with Spicy Peanut Sauce (p. 208), Hoisin Sauce (p. 206), and tahini. MAKES 36 SKEWERS.

Old-Fashioned Easy Meatloaf

My mother used to place three or four hard boiled eggs down the centre of the loaf before baking for an attractive and tasty presentation. Serve with mashed potatoes and Lynnie's Green Beans with Nami Sauce (page 75) for a real comfort food meal.

2 lbs (1 kg) lean ground beef, chicken, or turkey 1 egg 1 small onion, grated 3/4 cup (175 mL) bread crumbs 1 tsp (5 mL) Worcestershire sauce 1/2 tsp (2 mL) salt 1/2 tsp (2 mL) pepper	Mix all ingredients.
2/3 cup (150 mL) tomato juice	Add this last, and only enough to shape into a loaf. Put into Pyrex loaf pan. Bake at 375°F (190°C) for 1 1/2 hours.
	Serves 6.

Sweet and Sour Meatballs

Great with noodles or rice and a steamed vegetable.

1 large onion, diced 1 tbsp (15 mL) canola oil	Sauté onion in oil until light brown.
1 tbsp (15 mL) brown sugar 1 can (28 oz/796 mL) whole tomatoes 1 can (14 oz/398 mL) tomato sauce Juice of 1/2 lemon	Add sugar and stir, then add whole tomatoes, tomato sauce, and lemon juice. Boil gently until mixture is a runny sauce.
2 lbs (1 kg) lean ground beef, chicken, or turkey 1 egg 3 tbsp (50 mL) bread crumbs 2 tbsp (25 mL) ketchup 2 tbsp (25 mL) water 1 tsp (5 mL) Worcestershire sauce 1/2 tsp (2 mL) salt 1/2 tsp (2 mL) pepper	Mix well and form into small meatballs. Drop meatballs into boiling sauce and reduce to simmer. Cover pot and cook 1 1/2 hours.
Extra brown sugar Extra fresh lemon juice	Season at end with brown sugar and lemon juice. SERVES 6–8.

Salmon Patties

Serve with Tzatziki (page 207) and Colourful Jasmine Rice (page 236) or mashed potatoes and steamed vegetables or corn for the perfect comfort food.

I sometimes mix ½ cup (125 mL) corn niblets right in with the salmon mixture. My mom used to do this.

2 cans (each ½ oz/184 g) salmon 2 eggs ½ cup (125 mL) whole wheat bread crumbs ¼ cup (50 mL) chopped sweet onion 2 tbsp (25 mL) cornmeal ¼ tsp (1 mL) salt ¼ tsp (1 mL) black pepper	Mix together. Form patties.
½ cup (125 mL) bread crumbs (optional)	Dip into crumbs.
Canola oil	Preheat skillet; add small amount of oil (about 1½ tsp). Fit patties into pan. Cook until medium brown on both sides.
	SERVES 4.

Low-Cal Tuna Patties

These tuna patties serve four for dinner. Serve with Tzatziki (page 207) or you can melt some grated Cheddar on top for an extra special treat!

2 cans (each 6 oz/184 g) tuna	Drain and rinse tuna.
½ small sweet onion, chopped fine 1 egg ¼ cup (50 mL) celery, chopped ¼ tsp (1 mL) dry mustard ¼ tsp (1 mL) dry sage ¼ tsp (1 mL) low-sodium soy sauce 1 garlic clove, crushed Salt and pepper to taste	Combine with tuna and form 8 patties.
1 cup (250 mL) Japanese bread crumbs (panko) or bread crumbs	Roll patties in crumbs.
1 tbsp canola oil (optional)	Put in a greased 13- X 9-inch (3.5 L) casserole dish and bake at 375°F (190°C) for 15–20 minutes, or, fry in oil in a heated skillet until browned on both sides.
	SERVES 4.

Crab Cakes with Tropical Fresh-Fruit Salsa

Serve with Tropical Fresh-Fruit Salsa (recipe below).

1 lb (500 g) crabmeat, preferably Dungeness	Mix together and form 4 large or 8 small patties.
1 egg	
1/4 cup (50 mL) chopped sweet onion	
1/4 cup (50 mL) chopped celery	
1/4 cup (50 mL) Japanese bread crumbs (panko)	
2 tbsp (25 mL) mayonnaise	
1 tbsp (15 mL) Dijon mustard	
2 dashes Tabasco sauce	
Juice of 1 lemon	
1/4 tsp (1 mL) salt	
1/4 tsp (1 mL) black pepper	
1/2 cup Japanese bread crumbs (panko) (optional)	Dip both sides of patties into crumbs.
Small amount of canola oil or butter	Preheat frypan. Pour in oil. Fit patties into pan. Cook until medium brown on both sides.
	Serves 4.

Tropical Fresh-Fruit Salsa

1/2 cup (125 mL) diced pineapple	Combine in bowl. Refrigerate until ready to serve.
1/2 cup (125 mL) diced mango	
1/2 cup (125 mL) diced apple	
1/2 cup (125 mL) diced strawberries	Makes about 2 1/2 cups (625 mL).
1/2 cup (125 mL) seeded and diced red or yellow pepper	
2 tbsp (25 mL) rice vinegar	
1 tbsp (15 mL) minced cilantro	
1 tbsp (15 mL) granulated sugar	
1/4 tsp (1 mL) crushed red pepper flakes (optional)	

Colourful Jasmine Rice

If you can't find Thai basil, any fresh basil will work. The Thai basil adds an extra fragrance for me. Thai jasmine rice is a long-grain variety of rice. It's especially great with fish and chicken.

2 cups (500 mL) jasmine rice	Rinse in cold water then drain well.
2½ cups (625 mL) cold water	Put rice and cold water into saucepan with lid and bring to a boil. Reduce heat and simmer covered for about 5 minutes, or until all the water has evaporated. (Rice should be cooked through but slightly firm.)
2 tbsp (25 mL) olive oil ¼ cup (50 mL) finely chopped onion	In skillet, heat oil and sauté until the onion is transparent.
¼ cup (50 mL) finely chopped, peeled apple ¼ cup (50 mL) seeded and finely diced red pepper 2 tbsp (25 mL) finely diced orange segments	Add rest of ingredients and cook 30 seconds over high heat. Remove from heat. Combine with rice.
3 tbsp (50 mL) finely chopped fresh Thai basil Salt and pepper to taste	Add the basil and seasoning to rice and mix well. SERVES 8.

Mira's Favourite Coleslaw

It just gets better with age. This will last several days in the refrigerator until it's time to make more.

Dressing: ¾ cup (175 mL) mayonnaise ¼ cup (50 mL) white vinegar ¼ cup (50 mL) granulated sugar 2 tsp (10 mL) salt ¼ tsp (2 mL) black pepper	Mix all ingredients together. Blend well.
10 medium carrots, peeled 1 medium green cabbage ½ medium red cabbage 1 small sweet onion 1 red pepper, seeded	Finely shred all the vegetables in a food processor. Add the dressing and mix well. Let stand in refrigerator 2–4 hours before serving.
½ cup (125 mL) sunflower seeds, toasted (optional)	Add for extra crunch! SERVES 8.

Stuffed Baked Potatoes

A great comfort food lunch for kids who come home from school and a good way to use up leftover chicken or potatoes from the night before.

4 large potatoes	Bake potatoes in 350°F (180°C) oven for 1 hour, or until soft inside. Cut in half and scoop out potato into bowl.
¾ cup (175 mL) grated cheese 4 tbsp (60 mL) butter	Add to potato in bowl.
1–2 tbsp (15–25 mL) 2% milk	Add enough milk to soften mixture.
½ cup (125 mL) chopped cooked chicken ½ cup (125 mL) frozen peas, thawed	Add to potato mixture. Stuff potato skins with mixture. Return to oven for 15 minutes.
	Serves 4.

Variations for Stuffed Baked Potatoes:

Pizza Filling	Mix 4 oz (100 g) chopped salami, 6 oz (175 g) grated mozzarella cheese, and 2 tbsp (25 mL) grated Parmesan cheese into potato mixture. Top with 1 cup (250 mL) tomato sauce.
Taco Filling	Mix ½ of a 19 oz (540 mL) can red kidney beans, ½ cup (125 mL) grated Cheddar cheese, ½ cup (125 mL) sour cream, and ¼ cup (50 mL) crushed taco chips into potato mixture. Top with 1 cup (250 mL) salsa.

Aunt Naomi's Buttermilk Kugel

Serve with fresh berries and yogurt or light sour cream.
This is perfect for a Sunday brunch!

1 lb (500 g) dry egg noodles	Cook according to package directions. Drain well.
4 eggs ½ cup (125 mL) granulated sugar 2 tbsp (30 mL) butter	Mix together and add to noodles. Pour into 13- x 9-inch (3.5L) Pyrex dish.
4 cups (1L) buttermilk	Pour buttermilk over noodle mixture. Bake at 350°F (180°C) for 35 minutes.
1 cup (250 mL) cornflakes, crushed ⅓ cup (75 mL) brown sugar 2 tbsp (25 mL) melted butter	Mix together with fingers and sprinkle over top. Lower oven temperature to 325°F (160°C) and bake an additional 30 minutes.
	SERVES 8–10.

Spanakopita Logs

This recipe is the only way that I can get my daughter to eat spinach!

2 large bunches of fresh spinach	Wash and stem spinach, then steam or microwave until just wilted. Rinse with cold water. Squeeze out excess liquid. Chop.
1 onion, chopped 2 tbsp (25 mL) olive oil	Sauté onion in olive oil until soft.
½ lb (250 g) feta cheese, crumbled 3 eggs ¼ cup (125 mL) chopped fresh mint, (optional) 3 tbsp (50 mL) bread crumbs ¼ tsp (1 mL) salt ¼ tsp (1 mL) pepper Pinch of nutmeg	Mix together and add with onions to spinach.
Pastry: 12 oz (350 g) phyllo pastry 3 tbsp (50 mL) butter	Brush 4 sheets of phyllo lightly with butter and place on top of each other. Put spinach along the length of the phyllo on the edge. Seal by folding the sides ½ inch (1 cm) towards the centre, then roll up. Brush top with butter. Repeat with remaining phyllo. Bake in 425°F (220°C) oven for 20 minutes until brown and crispy. Cut each log into 4.
	SERVES 8.

Squash Brûlée

A terrific way to eat squash and to try different kinds of squash.
Thanks to Rena for the recipe, which we have at least once a week!

2 lb (1 kg) acorn or butternut squash, peeled and cubed 10 cups (2.5 L) water	Boil squash in water for 10 minutes. Drain squash.
1 egg ½ cup (125 mL) light cream ½ tsp (2 mL) nutmeg	Mash squash and mix with egg, cream, and nutmeg. Pour into 9-inch (22 cm) deep dish ceramic pie plate.
1 tbsp (15 mL) butter	Dot with butter. Bake at 350°F (180°C) for 20 minutes.
2 tbsp (25 mL) brown sugar	Press sugar through sieve and sprinkle lightly on top of cooked squash casserole. Place under broiler 2 minutes until golden.
	SERVES 6–8.

Mama Rozzie's
Green Bean Casserole

It's kind of old fashioned, but it was the only way Mom could get us to eat green beans.

2 lbs (1 kg) frozen green beans 1 can (10 oz/284 mL) cream of mushroom soup	Mix together beans and soup. Turn into buttered 13- x 9-inch (3.5 L) casserole.
1 can French-fried onion rings	Top with onion rings. Bake at 350°F (180°C) for 30–35 minutes.
	SERVES 6–8.

Tuna-Pineapple Pita Pockets

Pita pockets are fun for school lunches and can be filled with your child's favourite vegetables, meat, and cheeses.

1 can (4 oz/113 g) tuna, drained	Mix all ingredients together.
1 can (8 oz/250 g) crushed pineapple, drained	
$\frac{1}{4}$ cup (50 mL) shredded green or red cabbage	
2 oz (50 g) Cheddar cheese, grated	
2 tbsp (25 mL) mayonnaise	
8 pitas	Fill pita pockets with tuna mixture. Place in casserole dish and cover. Bake in oven at 325°F (160°C) for 15 minutes, or until centres are warm, or microwave, uncovered, for 90 seconds on High.
	MAKES 8 PITA POCKETS.

Easy Pita Pizzas

This is a delightful way to include the family in preparing their own meals. Pita pizzas are easy and nutritious.

4 whole wheat pitas 1 cup (250 mL) tomato sauce	Put ¼ cup (50 mL) of sauce on top of each pita.
2 tomatoes, sliced ½ red pepper, seeded and chopped ½ green pepper, seeded and chopped 8 slices salami or pepperoni 8 slices turkey	Let each family member add his or her own toppings.
6–8 oz (150–200 g) mozzarella cheese, grated ¼ cup (50 mL) grated Parmesan cheese	Top each pizza with cheese.
	Put pizzas on baking sheet. Bake at 450°F (230°C) for 10 minutes, or until bubbly. MAKES 4 PIZZAS.

Beef Tostadas on Tortillas

These can be a bit messy, but that's part of the fun!

1 tbsp (15 mL) olive oil ¼ cup (50 mL) finely chopped onion	Sauté onion in oil until translucent.
1 lb (500 g) ground beef or refried beans	Add beef or beans to onion and stir until cooked completely. Drain off excess fat.
⅓ cup (75 mL) chili sauce	Add to meat or bean mixture and stir.
8 corn tortillas	Heat tortillas in oven at 350°F (180°C) for 5 minutes, or until warm. Spoon ⅛ of meat or bean mixture onto each tortilla.
2 tomatoes, chopped ½ head lettuce, chopped in strips 6 oz (150 g) Cheddar cheese, grated 1 cup (250 mL) salsa	Use as toppings for each tortilla. Roll up and serve.
	MAKES 8 TOSTADAS.

Fettucine Lasagna

This is one of the most popular items for sale at The Lazy Gourmet. It's much easier and faster to make than traditional lasagnas, but every bit as delicious.

3½ cups (875 mL) tomato sauce	Use canned sauce or make your own (see page 247).
1½ lbs (750 g) fresh or 1 lb (500 g) dry fettucine	Cook pasta in boiling water for 5–6 minutes for fresh pasta; 8–10 minutes for dry. Set aside.
4 oz (100 g) mozzarella cheese, grated 4 oz (100 g) Swiss cheese, grated ½ cup (125 mL) grated Parmesan cheese	Mix cheeses together. Divide into two portions. Set aside.
2 eggs, beaten 1½ cup (375 mL) ricotta cheese Pinch nutmeg Salt and pepper to taste	Mix together and set aside.
	In large bowl, combine tomato sauce, noodles, and one portion of cheese mixture. Put half of this mixture into 13- x 9-inch (3.5 L) casserole dish. Spoon ricotta cheese–egg mixture over noodles. Top with remaining tomato sauce, cheese, and pasta mixture and sprinkle with second portion of cheese mixture. Bake at 30–35 minutes at 350°F (180°C), or until bubbly. SERVES 8.

Quick Tomato Sauce

This is a quick and easy way to make a delicious tomato sauce. Use it for any kind of pasta, tacos, or chili.

1–2 tbsp (15 mL) olive oil 1 onion, chopped	In large saucepan, sauté onion in oil for 4–5 minutes.
3 cloves garlic, minced	Add to onion and sauté for about 30 seconds.
½ cup (125 mL) water 2 carrots, peeled and grated 1 can (19 oz/540 mL) crushed tomatoes 3 tbsp (50 mL) tomato paste 1 tsp (5 mL) dried basil ¼ tsp (1 mL) dried oregano Pinch dried thyme	Add to saucepan and cook for 30 minutes. Purée in blender.
	MAKES 2 CUPS (500 ML).

Quick and Simple Chili Con Carne

Kids seem to love this recipe.

1 tbsp (15 mL) vegetable oil 1 lb (500 g) ground beef or pork 2 cloves garlic, minced	In large skillet, sauté beef and garlic in oil until thoroughly cooked. Drain off excess fat.
1 can (14 oz/398 mL) red kidney beans, drained and rinsed 1½ cups (375 mL) tomato sauce ¼ cup (50 mL) tomato paste 1 tsp (4–5 mL) chili powder	Add to meat and cook over medium heat for 20–25 minutes.
	Serve with corn chips or corn bread. SERVES 8.

Crispy Fish Fillets

Kids like crispy foods and this is one way to get them excited about fish.

6 snapper, cod, or halibut fillets 2 eggs, beaten Pinch each salt and pepper	Season the eggs with salt and pepper. Dip fillets into seasoned eggs.
1 cup (250 mL) cornflake crumbs or bread crumbs	Coat fillets with crumbs.
2–3 tbsp (50 mL) vegetable oil	Fry fillets in oil for 3 minutes on each side, or until golden brown.
	Serve with wedges of lemon and Cucumber and Dill Sauce (recipe follows). MAKES 6 FILLETS.

Cucumber and Dill Sauce

This is a light flavourful sauce that kids love for dipping or as a condiment.

1 cup (250 mL) plain yogurt $\frac{1}{3}$ cup (75 mL) grated English cucumber $\frac{1}{2}$ tsp (2 mL) fresh dill $\frac{1}{4}$ tsp (1 mL) salt	Mix together and serve with fish.
	MAKES APPROXIMATELY $1\frac{1}{2}$ CUPS (375 mL).

Our Family's Favourite Chicken

This is everyone's favourite chicken dish. I rarely tell anyone at the time how easy this recipe is as I always get rave reviews for it.

1 chicken, skinned and cut in serving pieces ½ bottle (8 oz/250 mL) salad dressing, any kind	Coat chicken in salad dressing.
¾–1 cup (175–250 mL) cornflake crumbs	Dip chicken pieces into crumbs one at a time and place in roasting pan. Bake at 375°F (190°C) for 1 hour, or until chicken is tender.
	SERVES 4–6.

Lyla's Cranberry Chicken

A Friday-night special year-round. Lyla has become famous nationwide for this recipe. It was originally published in my official Expo '86 souvenir cookbook and in sister Lynnie's runaway best seller, Chicken! Chicken! Chicken!

1 can (14 oz/398 mL) whole cranberry sauce ⅓ cup (75 mL) liquid honey ¼ cup (50 mL) orange juice concentrate ¼ cup (50 mL) low-sodium soy sauce	Combine ingredients in medium saucepan and bring to boil. Reduce heat and simmer for 5 minutes.
4 lb (2 kg) chicken, skinned and cut in serving pieces	Pour sauce over chicken and bake at 375°F (190°C) for 1 hour. Turn occasionally. The longer you cook it, the stickier it gets.
	SERVES 4–6.

Pizza Dough

With a pizza dough recipe, you can make great individual pizzas any time. Feel free to add herbs and cheese to make a simple focaccia bread.

1 ⅓ cups (325 mL) warm water 1 tbsp (15 mL) granulated sugar	Dissolve sugar in warm water.
1 pkg active dry yeast	Add yeast to sugared water and let stand for 5 minutes.
3 cups (750 mL) all-purpose flour 2 tbsp (25 mL) vegetable oil 1 tsp (5 mL) salt	Stir into yeast mixture to form dough. Knead until smooth and elastic.
	Place dough in oiled bowl and turn to coat all surfaces. Cover with oiled waxed paper and let sit in warm place for 1 hour, or until doubled. Punch down and stretch to fit 14-inch (35 cm) pizza pan or cookie sheet. Top with your favourite sauce (tomato or pesto) and your favourite cheeses and toppings. Bake at 400°F (200°C) for 20 minutes, or until bubbly.

MAKES ONE 14-INCH (35 CM) PIZZA CRUST.

Whole Wheat Pizza Dough

Whole wheat pizza has a heartier texture but one feels morally superior for making it!

1 ¼ cups (300 mL) warm water 1 tsp (5 mL) granulated sugar	Dissolve sugar in warm water.
1 pkg active dry yeast	Add yeast to sugared water and let stand for 5 minutes.
1 ¼ cups (300 mL) all-purpose flour 1 ¼ cups (300 mL) whole wheat flour 1 tsp (5 mL) salt	Mix together.
5 tbsp (75 mL) vegetable oil	Combine yeast mixture, flour, and oil. Knead until smooth and elastic. If dough sticks to bowl, add a bit more flour; if it's too dry, add some water, 1 tsp (5 mL) at a time.
	Transfer dough to greased bowl and turn to coat all sides with oil. Cover and let stand in a warm spot for 1 hour, or until doubled in volume. Punch down and stretch to fit 14-inch (35 cm) pizza pan or cookie sheet. Note: After the dough has risen, you can refrigerate it for up to three days. MAKES ONE 14-INCH (35 CM) PIZZA CRUST.

Fantasy Party Pizzas

Pizzas are the ultimate application of the food guide! You can combine all four food groups into one delicious and nutritious serving.

Pizza Dough (p. 250) or Whole Wheat Pizza Dough (p. 251) or dough for 14-inch (35 cm) pizza 2 cups (500 mL) grated cheese, any kind 1 cup (250 mL) tomato sauce	Roll out dough to fit 14-inch (35 cm) pizza pan or cookie sheet. Spread cheese and tomato sauce on pizza crust.
Red peppers, seeded and chopped Green peppers, seeded and chopped Mushrooms, sliced Tomatoes, sliced Pineapple, chopped Pepperoni or salami, sliced Sun-dried tomatoes, chopped Eggplant, sliced Olives	Let the children choose their own toppings.
	Bake in 425°F (220°C) oven on bottom rack for about 15 minutes, or until bubbly. MAKES 1 PIZZA.

Pizza Sauce

The longer you cook this, the thicker the sauce will be. Just make sure to stir it so it doesn't burn.

2 tbsp (25 mL) olive oil	Heat oil in saucepan.
2½ lbs (1.25 kg) fresh tomatoes, chopped	Add to oil and sauté.
¼ cup (50 mL) tomato paste 1 small carrot, peeled and grated 2 tbsp (25 mL) minced fresh basil or 1 tsp (5 mL) dried basil 1 tsp (5 mL) granulated sugar ½ tsp (2 mL) dried thyme ½ tsp (2 mL) dried oregano ½ tsp (2 mL) red pepper flakes 1 clove garlic, minced Salt and pepper to taste	Add vegetables, sugar, and herbs to tomatoes and cook, stirring occasionally, for 35–45 minutes.
	MAKES 1½–2 CUPS (375 TO 500 ML).

Pesto Sauce

Basil and parsley are loaded with beta carotene, vitamin C, and other vitamins. Use this sauce on pastas, pizzas, or quesadillas and in soups. Your kids are sure to love it.

3 cups (750 mL) fresh basil leaves 1 cup (250 mL) fresh parsley sprigs 4 cloves garlic, minced ½ cup (125 mL) grated Parmesan cheese ½ cup (125 mL) toasted pine nuts or walnuts	Using blender or food processor, process until ingredients are thoroughly mixed.
1 cup (250 mL) olive oil	Add oil to herb mixture gradually, continuing to process, until a creamy paste is formed.
Salt and pepper to taste	Season with salt and pepper.
	Makes 1½–2 cups (375–500 mL).

Four-Cheese Pizza

Feel free to experiment with any four cheeses. This was our favourite combo.

Dough for 14-inch (35 cm) pizza	Roll out dough to fit 14-inch (35 cm) pizza pan or cookie sheet.
2 oz (50 g) mozzarella cheese, grated 2 oz (50 g) Camembert (include rind), thinly sliced 2 oz (50 g) Parmesan cheese, grated 2 oz (50 g) feta cheese, crumbled	Mix together.
1 cup (250 mL) tomato sauce	Spread sauce over crust. Top with cheeses. Bake at 475°F (240°C) for 20 minutes, or until bubbly.
	Serves 2–4.

Nuts and Bolts Mix

Great to keep around the house for a nutritious snack.

3 cups (750 mL) bite-sized shredded wheat cereal	Mix together and keep in jars for quick snacks.
3 cups (750 mL) Cheerios or 2 cups (500 mL) thin pretzels, broken into smaller pieces	
2 cups (500 mL) roasted peanuts	
	Makes 7–8 cups (1.75–2 L).

Oatmeal Cookies

Feel free to add carob or chocolate chips, coconut, or walnuts.

¾ cup (175 mL) brown sugar	Cream sugar and margarine well.
½ cup (125 mL) margarine	
1 egg, beaten	Add to sugar and margarine.
½ cup (125 mL) 2% milk	Add to egg mixture. Set aside.
2 cups (500 mL) all-purpose flour	Sift flour, soda, and salt into bowl. Combine with egg mixture and mix well.
1 tsp (5 mL) baking soda	
½ tsp (2 mL) salt	
2 cups (500 mL) quick-cooking rolled oats	Add to flour mixture and stir well.
1 cup (250 mL) raisins	
	Drop by rounded teaspoonfuls (5 mL) onto cookie sheets. Bake at 350°F (180°C) for 12 minutes, or until golden brown.
	Makes 3 dozen cookies.

Dad's Oatmeal Cookies

Feel free to add nuts or carob chips or raisins or dried fruit to this recipe!

1 1/2 cups (375 mL) all-purpose flour 1 tsp (5 mL) baking powder 1 tsp (5 mL) baking soda 1/2 tsp (2 mL) salt	Sift and set aside.
1 1/4 cups (300 mL) brown sugar 2/3 cup (150 mL) margarine or butter	Beat until fluffy.
2 eggs 1 tsp (5 mL) vanilla	Add eggs to butter-sugar mixture one at a time. Beat well after each addition. Add vanilla. Add flour mixture.
1 1/2 cups (375 mL) quick-cooking rolled oats 1 cup (250 mL) shredded sweetened coconut	Add oats and coconut. Roll into balls and flatten with back of fork. Bake at 350°F (180°C) 12–15 minutes.
	MAKES 60 COOKIES.

Soft Ginger Cookies with Oatmeal

Imagine, a delicious ginger cookie with the added nutrition of oats!

2 cups (500 mL) all-purpose flour 2 tsp (10 mL) ground ginger 3/4 tsp (3 mL) ground cinnamon 1/2 tsp (2 mL) ground cloves 1/2 tsp (2 mL) baking soda 1/4 tsp (1 mL) salt	Sift together.
1 cup (250 mL) quick-cooking rolled oats	Add to above and set aside.
3/4 cup (180 mL) margarine 1 cup (250 mL) granulated sugar	Cream margarine and add sugar gradually.
1 egg	Beat into mixture.
1 tbsp (15 mL) cold water 1/4 cup (50 mL) molasses	Stir into above.
2 tbsp (30 mL) superfine sugar	Add dry ingredients. Mix until well blended. Shape dough into walnut-sized balls and roll in superfine sugar. Flatten slightly. Bake at 350°F (180°C) for 8–10 minutes.
	MAKES 48 COOKIES.

The Brook Sisters'
Flax Spelt Oatmeal Chippers

These are the most popular cookies that we now sell at The Lazy Gourmet. Our customers were ready for a cookie that is filled with nutrition!

¹/₂ cup (125 mL) butter ¹/₃ cup (75 mL) margarine ¹/₂ cup (125 mL) brown sugar 1 tsp (5 mL) vanilla ¹/₂ tsp (2 mL) cinnamon	Cream together until smooth.
¹/₂ cup (125 mL) large rolled oats ¹/₂ cup (125 mL) quick-cooking oats ¹/₂ cup (150 mL) whole wheat flour ¹/₂ cup (125 mL) organic spelt flour ¹/₂ tsp (2 mL) baking soda ¹/₂ cup (125 mL) freshly ground flax seeds, also known as flaxmeal ³/₄ cup (175 mL) miniature chocolate chips	One at a time, add these items (sift soda with flours).
	Roll into logs. Chill 2 hours then slice into ¹/₂" (1 cm) pieces. Arrange on cookie sheets (sprayed with cooking spray) and bake at 350°F (180°C) for 12 minutes.
	MAKES 36 COOKIES.

Optional Additions:

chopped sun-dried cherries

chopped dried mango (not if also using chocolate)

chopped walnuts or pecans

sweetened shredded or flaked coconut

sunflower seeds

dried cranberries

Poppyseed Oatmeal Cookies

I like these very thin. Some people like them thicker. Play with the recipe to find your preference.

2¹/₂ cups (625 mL) all-purpose flour 1 tsp (5 mL) baking powder ¹/₄ tsp (1 mL) salt	Sift together.
2 cups (500 mL) quick-cooking rolled oats ¹/₂ cup (125 mL) poppyseeds	Add to flour mixture. Set aside.
¹/₂ cup (125 mL) butter ¹/₂ cup (125 mL) canola oil	Cream butter and oil well.
1 cup (250 mL) brown sugar ¹/₃ cup (75 mL) granulated sugar	Gradually add sugars and beat until fluffy.
1 egg	Add and beat until light.
¹/₄ cup (60 mL) milk 1 tsp (5 mL) vanilla	Add to butter-sugar mixture.
	Add dry ingredients until well blended. Roll out on floured board. Cut into shapes. Place on baking sheet. Bake at 350°F (180°C) 10–12 minutes until light brown. MAKES 3 DOZEN COOKIES.

Peanut Butter Brownies

These are a terrific brownie with the benefit of peanut butter to add some protein. Not a snack to be made every day but good for the occasional treat.

³/₄ cup (175 mL) margarine ²/₃ cup (150 mL) semisweet chocolate chips	Heat together until just melted. Set aside.
1¹/₄ cup (300 mL) granulated sugar 3 eggs, lightly beaten 1 tsp (5 mL) vanilla	Beat together.
³/₄ cup (180 g) all-purpose flour ¹/₃ cup (75 mL) cocoa 1 tsp (5 mL) baking powder	Sift together and add to egg mixture above. Add melted chocolate. Pour into 13- x 9-inch (3.5 L) pan sprayed with cooking spray.
¹/₄ cup (50 mL) semisweet chocolate chips ¹/₂ cup (125 mL) crunchy peanut butter (natural)	Mix together and drop by spoonfuls into mixture and swirl through with a knife. Bake about 35 minutes. Cool and cut into 32 pieces.
	MAKES 32 BROWNIES.

Peanut Butter and Honey Granola Bars

This is a snack loaded with fibre, vitamins, and minerals.

3 cups (750 mL) quick-cooking rolled oats 1 cup (250 mL) bran 1 cup (250 mL) dessicated unsweetened coconut 1 cup (250 mL) sunflower seeds ½ cup (125 mL) chopped almonds (optional) ½ cup (125 mL) raisins ¼ cup (50 mL) wheat germ	Mix dry ingredients in large bowl. Set aside.
½ cup (125 mL) liquid honey ½ cup (125 mL) vegetable oil ½ cup (125 mL) brown sugar ½ cup (125 mL) peanut butter	Combine in small saucepan and cook over medium-low heat until dissolved.
1 tbsp (15 mL) 2% milk 2 tsp (10 mL) vanilla ¾ tsp (4 mL) baking soda	Combine and add to honey mixture. Bring to a boil, then remove from heat.
	Pour honey-milk mixture over granola mixture and stir well. Wet your hands and press mixture into 15- x 10-inch (40 x 25 cm) jelly roll pan. Bake at 275°F (140°C) for 20–25 minutes. Cut into slices and store in refrigerator. MAKES 36 SQUARES.

Apple Crisp

This is an all-time favourite. Your kids will love to help make this crunchy dessert.

6 large apples, peeled and sliced	Arrange apples in greased 9-inch (2.5 L) square pan.
¼ cup (50 mL) water 1 tbsp (15 mL) lemon juice 1 tbsp (15 mL) cinnamon ½ tsp (2 mL) cloves	Mix together and sprinkle over apples. Set aside.
¾ cup (175 mL) all-purpose flour ½ cup (175 mL) brown sugar, packed ¾ cup (125 mL) quick-cooking rolled oats 6 tbsp (90 mL) butter	Rub together to form crumbs. Spread over apples.
	Bake at 350°F (180°C) for 35–40 minutes. Serve hot or cold. SERVES 6–8.

Peanut Butter Krispies

*Lots of nutrition packed into a great snack. These could last a
week if stored in an airtight container.*

1 cup (250 mL) corn syrup 1 cup (250 mL) brown sugar	Heat syrup and sugar in small saucepan until sugar is dissolved.
1 cup (250 mL) peanut butter	Add peanut butter to sugar mixture and stir until bubbles form.
3 cups (750 mL) Special K cereal 3 cups (750 mL) Rice Krispies cereal	Add to peanut butter mixture and stir well.
	Press into lightly oiled 13- x 9-inch (3.5 L) pan. Chill for 30 minutes before cutting into 24 squares. MAKES 24 SQUARES.

Snack Kit

*Take small amounts at a time in small bags for a quick energy
snack. It's also a great snack for adults!*

2 cups (500 mL) toasted nuts, any kind 1 cup (250 mL) sunflower seeds 1 cup (250 mL) dried prunes, apricots, and peaches $\frac{1}{2}$ cup (125 mL) raisins $\frac{1}{2}$ cup (125 mL) carob chips $\frac{1}{2}$ cup (125 mL) coconut	Mix together and store in a tightly covered jar.
	MAKES 5$\frac{1}{2}$ CUPS (1.25 L).

Rice Pudding

This recipe brings together three of the food groups. Add fruit and you've got them all.

4 cups (1 L) whole or 2% milk 1 cup (125 mL) long-grain rice ½ cup (125 mL) sugar ½ tsp (2 mL) salt ¼ tsp (1 mL) cinnamon Pinch nutmeg	Put into large saucepan. Cover and cook over low heat for 2 hours. Stir every 15 minutes.
2 egg yolks 2 tbsp (25 mL) water 1 tsp (5 mL) vanilla	Mix together egg yolks, water, and vanilla. Add 1 cup (250 mL) rice mixture to egg mixture. Return to pot and cook additional 4–5 minutes.
3–4 tbsp (60 mL) sugar 1 tbsp (15 mL) cinnamon	Combine well. Pour on top of pudding. Serve warm.
	SERVES 4.

Frozen Banana Pops

This is an obvious way to get your children involved in preparing a nutritious snack. It's easy to make and lots of fun to eat.

2 ripe bananas, peeled and cut in half 4 tbsp (60 mL) sweetened shredded coconut	Roll bananas in coconut.
	Carefully put popsicle stick into bananas. Wrap each pop in waxed paper, and freeze for at least 2–3 hours (overnight is better). MAKES 4 POPS.

Frozen Fruit Pops

1 $\frac{1}{2}$ tsp (7 mL) unflavoured gelatin 2 cups (500 mL) fruit juice	Sprinkle gelatin over $\frac{1}{2}$ cup (125 mL) fruit juice in small saucepan. Let stand 2 minutes. Stir over low heat until gelatin dissolves. Add remaining fruit juice and stir well. Remove from heat.
	Pour into popsicle moulds and freeze for 3 hours, or until firm. MAKES 6–8 POPS.

Everyday Frozen Pops

A kid's favourite to eat and to help make. It's a good idea to make them early in the day so that you will be able to enjoy them the same day.

2 cups (500 mL) fruit-flavoured yogurt 2 cups (500 mL) 2% milk	Combine and stir well.
	Pour into popsicle moulds. Put sticks into yogurt. Freeze overnight. MAKES EIGHT 4-OZ (100 G) POPS.

Easy Frozen Juice Pops

1 can (12 oz/341 mL) frozen fruit juice 2 cans water	Dilute concentrated juice with water. Pour into popsicle moulds and freeze 1 hour or until partially set. Put sticks into moulds. Freeze overnight.
	MAKES 16 POPS.

Frozen Pudding Sticks

4 oz (113 g) package instant pudding 4 cups (1 L) 2% milk, heated until very hot	Combine and stir well. Let return to room temperature.
	Pour pudding into popsicle moulds. When partially frozen add sticks. Freeze overnight. MAKES 16 POPS.

Milkshakes

Add fruit to milkshakes for extra flavour and nutrition.

2 scoops ice milk 1 cup (250 mL) cold 2% milk	Put milk and ice milk in blender and blend well. Pour into tall glass.
¼ cup (50 mL) blueberries ¼ cup (50 mL) raspberries ¼ cup (50 mL) strawberries ½ banana	Add any of these for a fruity flavour and blend.
	SERVES 1–2.

Banana Smoothie

Healthful snacks encourage good eating habits. It's a great snack for moms because it's full of calcium.

1 banana 1 cup (250 mL) 2% milk 1 cup (250 mL) ice cubes 2 tsp (10 mL) liquid honey ½ tsp (2 mL) vanilla	Process in blender until smooth. SERVES 1–2.

Peach Smoothie

1 cup (250 mL) drained canned peaches 1 cup (250 mL) ice cubes 1 cup (250 mL) vanilla yogurt ½ cup (125 mL) orange juice	Process in blender until smooth. SERVES 1–2.

Mixed Fruit Smoothie

1 cup (250 mL) fruit yogurt 1 cup (250 mL) ice cubes ½ cup (125 mL) fresh raspberries 1 ripe peach, pitted and sliced ½ banana	Process in blender until smooth. SERVES 1–2.

Party Sandwiches

Everyone loves party sandwiches but most people find them a pain to make. Get your kids to help and have them make up a big batch together on the weekend. Freeze them and let them choose each day which ones they want to take to school. Here are some great ideas for fillings and variations. It'll be a party for you all week!

Roll-up sandwiches

Ask the baker to slice your whole wheat and enriched white bread lengthwise. When you have your filling ready, use a rolling pin to gently press the bread down. This will make it easier to roll up and you will not tear the bread. Spread with filling and roll up tightly. Wrap with plastic wrap and chill overnight or freeze until ready to cut. Cut them at the last minute, as the bread tends to go stale quickly.

Ribbon sandwiches

Spread a slice of white bread with tuna, top with a slice of whole wheat bread, spread egg salad on the whole wheat slice, and top with another slice of white bread. Chill and cut into strips.

Triangle sandwiches

Use one kind of bread on the bottom and another on the top. Fill them and cut them into small triangles.

Cut-out sandwiches

These are cute and great for parties, but can be wasteful if much of the sandwich is left out of the cutter. If you can find good cutters that will use most of the sandwich, go ahead and have fun with them. We have a Mickey Mouse cutter that looks great and ensures minimal waste.

Sandwich Fillings and Spreads

Always serve with vegetable sticks and dips.

Egg salad
3 hard-cooked eggs
2 tbsp (25 mL) mayonnaise
Salt and pepper to taste

Homemade cheese spread
1 cup (250 mL) grated Cheddar cheese
½ cup (125 mL) cream cheese

Pineapple cheese spread
½ cup (125 mL) cream cheese
½ cup (125 mL) crushed pineapple

Tuna or salmon salad
1 can (7½ oz/213 mL) tuna or salmon
4 tbsp (50 mL) mayonnaise
2 tbsp (25 mL) toasted sunflower seeds (optional)
2 tsp (5 mL) lemon juice

Party Pita Pockets

Have the pitas precut so that the kids can see the pockets. Put a variety of fillings on the table and let the kids fill up the pocket with their favourites. Don't have too many different choices—it will only confuse them.

Sliced or chopped or grated cheeses
Sliced tomatoes
Shredded lettuce
Chopped cucumbers
Egg salad
Tuna salad
Peanut butter and jam
Hummus and tahini

Canada's Food Guide to Healthy Eating

CANADA'S

Food Guide

TO HEALTHY EATING
FOR PEOPLE FOUR YEARS
AND OVER

Different People Need Different Amounts of Food

The amount of food you need every day from the 4 food groups and other foods depends on your age, body size, activity level, whether you are male or female and if you are pregnant or breast-feeding. That's why the Food Guide gives a lower and higher number of servings for each food group. For example, young children can choose the lower number of servings, while male teenagers can go to the higher number. Most other people can choose servings somewhere in between.

Grain Products

5 – 12
SERVINGS PER DAY

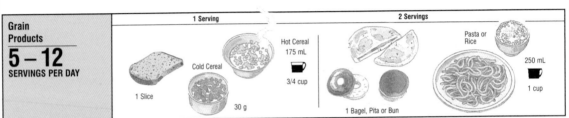

1 Serving — Cold Cereal, 30 g; 1 Slice; Hot Cereal 175 mL, 3/4 cup
2 Servings — 1 Bagel, Pita or Bun; Pasta or Rice, 250 mL, 1 cup

Vegetables and Fruit

5 – 10
SERVINGS PER DAY

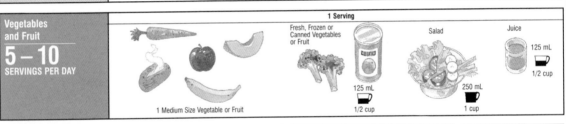

1 Serving — 1 Medium Size Vegetable or Fruit; Fresh, Frozen or Canned Vegetables or Fruit, 125 mL, 1/2 cup; Salad, 250 mL, 1 cup; Juice, 125 mL, 1/2 cup

Milk Products

SERVINGS PER DAY
Children 4–9 years: 2–3
Youth 10–16 years: 3–4
Adults: 2–4
Pregnant and Breast-feeding
Women 3–4

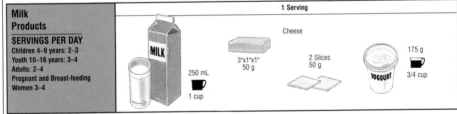

1 Serving — MILK, 250 mL, 1 cup; Cheese, 3"x1"x1", 50 g; 2 Slices, 50 g; YOGOURT, 175 g, 3/4 cup

Meat and Alternatives

2 – 3
SERVINGS PER DAY

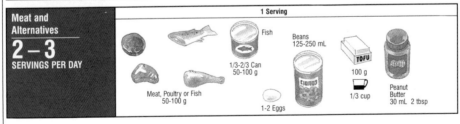

1 Serving — Meat, Poultry or Fish, 50-100 g; Fish, 1/3-2/3 Can, 50-100 g; 1-2 Eggs; Beans 125-250 mL, 1/3 cup; TOFU, 100 g; Peanut Butter, 30 mL 2 tbsp

Other Foods

Taste and enjoyment can also come from other foods and beverages that are not part of the 4 food groups. Some of these foods are higher in fat or Calories, so use these foods in moderation.

Acknowledgements

Many thanks to all the staff at The Lazy Gourmet for their support and help in this project. Also to my family, Jack, Mira, and Soleil, for putting up with all the chaos!

SUSAN MENDELSON

I would like to acknowledge the help and support of my husband, Allan Detsky, and my sons Michael and Jeffrey who taught me more about feeding children than any textbook. I would also like to thank Ryerson University and the faculty, staff, and students of the School of Nutrition, for making it possible for me to work on this book. Elias Chu deserves special mention for typing the earliest drafts of the project.

RENA MENDELSON

Index

A

alcohol, and pregnancy, 6–7
allergic reactions:
    and breast-feeding, 123
    to formula, 134
    and introducing solid foods, 138–39
anemia:
    and folate deficiency, 21
    and iron deficiency, 18–19, 20, 146,
        188–89
    and vitamin B_{12} deficiency, 21, 23
anorexia nervosa, 4, 179
antacids, 27–28
appetite:
    in babies, 124, 135, 141, 145
    and children's growth, 146, 148, 165,
        176–77, 197–98
    during pregnancy, 11–12
    spoilers, 169–70, 174, 177, 178
aversions, during pregnancy, 30

B

beta carotene, 37, 167
    and hypercarotenemia, 142
birth control:
    and nutrition, 5–6
    while breast-feeding, 129
birth defects:
    and iodine, 25
    and isotretinoin, 26
    and zinc, 24
birth weight:
    effects of smoking on, 8
    risks of low, 8
blood glucose, and breakfast, 171–72
Body Mass Index (BMI):
    chart, 10
    and healthy weight gain, 9–11
bone mass:
    and calcium, 14, 189
    and young mothers, 15
bottle feeding:
    about, 134–35
    supplement to nursing, 130
    timing of, 135
    vs. breast-feeding, 121–25
botulism, 144
breakfast, importance of, 171–72
breast pumps, 133
breast-feeding:
    and bottle feeding, 121–25, 130
    and exercise, 129–30
    how to provide milk, 125–26

and maternal weight gain, 12–13,
    128–30
    problems with, 124
    returning to work, 132–33
    when to stop, 133
bulimia, 4
burping, necessity of, 126, 135

C

caffeine, 27
calcium:
    and bone mass, 189–90
    need for while pregnant, 14–17
    requirements while pregnant, 17
    sources of, 17, 190
    supplements, 17, 191
calories:
    and breast-feeding, 35, 128–29
    need during pregnancy, 11, 35
Canada's Food Guide to Healthy Eating,
    272
    recommendations, 36, 37, 38, 161, 165,
        197
    requirements for pregnant or breast-
        feeing women, 35
Canadian Paediatric Nutrition
    Committee, 137, 140
cereal:
    for babies, 138, 140–41, 142, 147
    as breakfast food for children, 171, 172
cheese, and lactose, 16
child abuse, and alcohol consumption, 7
chocolate, and heartburn, 27
colic, 127, 136
colostrum, 125
constipation, and hormone levels, 28
cow's milk see milk
cravings, during pregnancy, 29–30
cretinism, 25
crying, 126, 135–36
cystic acne, 26

D

dairy products, and calcium, 14–16
dental caries *see* tooth decay
diet, and chronic disease, 161–62
dieting trends, 4

E

eating:
    disorders, 4, 179
    habits and tooth decay, 185–86
    in babies, 144–45

R

"restaurant syndrome," 197

S

salt, consumption, 25, 26–27
sandwiches, and school lunches, 174–75
saunas, during pregnancy, 32
school lunches, 174–76
scurvy risk, 26
seafood, introducing, 147
self-feeding, 143–44
serotonin, 186
smoking, effect on birth weight, 8
snacks, importance of, 147–48, 173–74
solid foods, readiness for, 138–43
soy formula, 134
spina bifida, and folic acid, 21
sports injuries, 32
steam baths, during pregnancy, 32
stress, during pregnancy, 31–32
sudden infant death syndrome (SIDS),
   and smoking, 8
sugar, 184–87
   and hyperactivity, 186–87
   obesity, 186
   and tooth decay, 185–86
supplements, multivitamin, 25–26
sweets, 184–85

T

taste, child's vs. adult's, 166–67
television:
   as appetite spoiler, 178, 183
   and food messages, 192–93
   and weight preoccupation, 179
thermal food jar, 175
tooth decay, and sweets, 184–86

V

vegetables, and calcium, 16–17
vegetarianism:
   and children, 191–92
   and vitamin B_{12}, 23–24

vitamin(s):
   and babies, 137
   supplements, 6, 129
vitamin A, 19
   and isotretinoin, 26
vitamin B_6, 23
vitamin B_{12}, 23–24
   deficiency, 21
   and vegetarianism, 23–24
vitamin C, and iron, 189
vitamin D:
   and breast-fed babies, 137
   and calcium, 189–90
vitamin K, 137
vomiting, coping with, 13

W

water, giving an infant, 131
water retention, 26–27
weaning, 133
weaning food(s), 138–43
   cereal, 138, 140–41, 142, 147
   how to feed, 140–43
   meat, 142
   to avoid, 143–44
weight gain:
   and pregnancy, 8–11
   in children
   and breakfast, 171
   healthy, 176–77
   obsession with, 178–80
wet nurses, 121
work, and breast-feeding, 132–33

Y

yogurt, and lactose intolerance, 16

Z

zinc:
   in diet, 20
   role in fetal development, 24–25

Index to Recipes